When the pews grow empty

Renewing Faith, Rebuilding Community, and Restoring the Mission of the Church

Edward Fair

Copyright © 2025 by Edward Fair

All rights reserved. No part of this book may be reproduced, stored in a retrieval system, or transmitted in any form or by any means electronic, mechanical, photocopying, recording, or otherwise without the prior written permission of the author, except in the case of brief quotations used in reviews or scholarly works.

This book is a work of nonfiction. Names, characters, places, and incidents are used truthfully. Any resemblance to actual persons, living or dead, outside of these factual references is purely coincidental.

Scripture quotations are taken from the Holy Bible, New International Version® (NIV®), unless otherwise noted. Used by permission. All rights reserved worldwide.

Published by Edward Fair

Cover design by Edward Fair

For information or inquiries, please contact:

Edward Fair

www.authoredwardfair.com

First Edition

Dedication
To God
the Creator of the universe, the Giver of life, and the Sustainer of all things.
Lord, this book is my humble offering to You,
born out of prayer, reflection, and a deep love for Your church.
You are the One who called me,
the One who sustained me through moments of doubt,
and the One who whispered truth when silence filled the pews.
I dedicate these words to You,
that they may point others to Your faithfulness,
awaken hearts to Your calling,
and remind us of all that You have not abandoned Your people.
May this work be used to inspire renewal,
to bring healing to broken places,
and to call Your church back to its first love.
Thank You for Your grace, for Your Word,
and for the privilege of serving in Your name.
To You alone be the glory
in the church, in the world, and forevermore.
Soli Deo Gloria (Glory to God Alone)

Introduction

For many churches today, the sight of empty pews is a stark reminder that something has shifted. Where there was once the comforting murmur of fellowship and the steady rhythm of worship, there is now an unsettling quiet. This book is born from the echoes of that silence a journey into the heart of why the pews are growing empty and how the church can rediscover its calling.

In these chapters, we will examine not only the challenges facing congregations but also the pathways toward renewal. We will explore the reasons people leave disconnection, division, doubt, and the ways churches can respond with humility, love, and courage. We will revisit the timeless mission of the church: to glorify God, make disciples, and serve the world. And we will offer practical solutions for leaders and members alike to nurture community, deepen discipleship, and extend radical hospitality.

This book is not just for pastors or church leaders it is for anyone who loves the church and longs to see it thrive. It is for those who sit in empty sanctuaries, wondering if hope stays. It is for those who feel disconnected or disillusioned but still long for authentic community. It is for those ready to move beyond despair into action.

The reflections and strategies offered here are not quick fixes or magic formulas. They are, instead, an invitation to return to the basics of faith prayer, Scripture, love, and service. They are rooted in a belief that God is not done with His church and that renewal is possible when we listen for His voice and follow His lead.

A Note on Scripture:

Throughout this book, I have quoted from the New International Version (NIV) of the Bible unless otherwise noted. The NIV strikes a balance between readability and faithfulness to the original text, making it accessible for a broad audience.

As you begin this journey, I invite you to open your heart to God's prompting. To read with both honesty and hope. To ask challenging questions, but also to seek His answers.

Let us pray for the wisdom and knowledge we will need on this path.

A Prayer for Wisdom and Knowledge:

Gracious and loving God,

We come before You with hearts eager to understand, minds longing for wisdom, and spirits seeking Your truth. As we journey through these pages, open our eyes to see what You see, open our ears to hear Your voice, and soften our hearts to receive Your correction and encouragement.

Grant us wisdom beyond our own, that we might discern the path forward for Your church. Fill us with knowledge not for pride or power, but for service and love. Remind us that the church is not ours but Yours, and that You are always faithful to build and rebuild Your kingdom.

Strengthen us to listen to those who are hurting, to welcome those who feel unseen, to disciple with grace, and to serve with humility. May the words of this book be used by Your Spirit to spark renewal, deepen faith, and restore hope in every congregation.

In Jesus' name, we pray. Amen.

Chapter One: The Echo of Silence

It was a Sunday morning unlike others, though it had not happened overnight. The sanctuary, once brimming with the sounds of whispered greetings, choir rehearsals, and the warm hum of conversation, now echoed with a silence so loud it filled the room. Where once rows of pews had been filled with familiar faces neighbors, family members, longtime friends there were now long stretches of empty seats. Only a few scattered congregants sat quietly, their heads bowed in silent reflection, the spaces between them a stark reminder of what was missing.

I stood at the back of the church, watching as the last few stragglers took their places. The organist struck the first chord of the prelude; a sound meant to stir the spirit and prepare hearts for worship. But today, the notes seemed to linger in the air, unanswered. Even the music seemed hesitant, unsure of its audience.

What had happened? How had this church once the heart of the community, once a bustling hub of faith and fellowship become a hollow shell of its former self? This was not just one congregation's story. Across the country, similar scenes were playing out. Sanctuaries sat quiet and empty. Pews grew dusty. The buzz of conversation after worship had dimmed to a few polite nods before people hurried back to their cars.

The reasons were many. Some were easy to name: changing demographics, the rise of secularism, the busyness of modern life. But beneath those explanations lay deeper wounds. People had been hurt by leaders, by rigid rules, by gossip and hypocrisy. Others had simply drifted, finding that church no longer met their needs or spoke to their hearts. For some, faith itself had not disappeared but the structures around it had felt increasingly irrelevant.

I remembered the stories shared over coffee and in quiet conversations stories of families who left after a disagreement with leadership, of young people who went off to college and never returned, of members who grew tired of church politics or bored with sermons that did not connect. I remembered the faces of those who once sang in the choir or volunteered at every church dinner but were now absent, their absence felt like a missing note in a familiar hymn.

And yet, in this silence, I also sensed a longing. A question that hung in the air like incense: Could these pews ever be full again? Could the church find its voice, its mission, its heart? Could we move beyond programs and performance and rediscover what it truly meant to be a community of faith?

I stood there, listening to the quiet hum of the air conditioner and the faint shuffle of hymnals being opened. And I realized this was not just an ending it could be a beginning. But first, we had to name the silence. We had to face the emptiness. Only then could we begin to ask what God was calling us to do next.

The echo of silence was not the end of the story. It was the moment where we stopped and listened really listened to what was left unsaid, to the cries of those who had left, and to the gentle whisper of a Spirit who had not given up on us yet.

I stood there, listening to the quiet hum of the air conditioner and the faint shuffle of hymnals being opened. And I realized this was not just an ending

it could be a beginning. But first, we had to name the silence. We had to face the emptiness. Only then could we begin to ask what God was calling us to do next.

But listening alone would not be enough. It was time to step beyond the walls of the church and into the spaces where our people had scattered. Instead of waiting for them to return on their own, what if we went to them?

We could start by rebuilding relationships. I thought of the names of those who had drifted away the young couple who stopped attending after their baby was born, the older man who withdrew after his wife passed, the family who felt overlooked when they asked for prayer and never heard back. What if I or any of us reached out, not with pressure or guilt, but with genuine care? A phone call, a handwritten note, an invitation for coffee. Small gestures of presence that say, "You still matter. We still care."

Next, we could reimagine what church could be. What if instead of focusing on filling pews, we focused on filling hearts? It is time for more small gatherings home groups, service projects, shared meals that build real community and meet people where they are. It is time to simplify the programs and re-center on the Gospel: love God, love people.

And, most importantly, we could pray differently. Instead of praying for numbers to increase or finances to improve, we could pray for a renewal of passion and purpose. We could ask God to break our hearts for the lost and give us courage to change what needs to change not for the sake of tradition, but for the sake of reaching the hurting, the lonely, and the searching.

I imagined what might happen if we stopped thinking of church as a place and started seeing it as a people people who live and love like Jesus, every day of the week. What if the echo of silence became the first note of a new song, one of hope and healing?

It was clear to me now. The solution would not come from a new program or a flashy marketing campaign. It would come from listening, reaching out, simplifying, and praying. It would come from hearts turned toward God and toward one another.

As I turned and walked down the aisle, I did not feel defeated. I felt called. Called to be part of the answer to the silence. Called to bring the love of Christ not just to the pews but to the people, wherever they may be.

The echo of silence may have begun the story, but with God's help, it will not be how it ends.

Chapter Two: The Generational Drift

When I was growing up, Sunday mornings were a family ritual. My parents dressed us in our best clothes, my father tied his favorite church tie, and we piled into the car. The sanctuary felt alive, filled with families like ours. Children squirmed in pews, grandparents whispered prayers, and teens whispered jokes. The church was not just a building it was part of life.

But now, many of those same sanctuaries sit half-empty, and it is hard to miss that a large part of the absent crowd is younger. Millennials, Gen Z, and even the emerging Gen Alpha have, in many cases, drifted away from church entirely.

I have heard the reasons, often repeated in conversations with parents and church leaders:

"They're too busy."

"They think church is boring or irrelevant."

"They prefer online content."

"They've been hurt or disillusioned by organized religion."

Some of these reasons sting because they feel like a rejection of what we have worked so hard to build. But others are honest indictments of a church that, in some cases, has not kept up with the shifting currents of culture and communication.

It is not just that young people are leaving it is that we did not always stop to ask why. We assumed they would come back when they got older, married, or had kids of their own. But many have not. Their absence has become the new normal, and now entire generations are growing up with no real connection to a faith community.

I remember talking with a college student who had grown up attending church every week. When I asked why she stopped going, she said, "I did not feel like I was part of anything bigger. It felt like everyone was just going through the motions. And honestly, I could find better conversations about God and life online than in the church lobby."

Her words stuck with me. It was not that she did not believe in God. It was that she had not found a community where her questions were welcome and her gifts could be used.

So, what do we do? Do we write off these generations as "lost," or do we listen more closely?

It is time to offer solutions, not excuses.

First, we must create spaces where young people feel heard, valued, and equipped. Instead of telling them to sit quietly in pews and wait their turn, we can invite them into real conversations about faith, culture, and purpose. We can let them lead worship, ask problematic questions, and contribute their unique perspectives.

Second, we can embrace technology as a tool, not a threat. Livestreams, social media, podcasts, and online Bible studies are not replacements for community, but they can be bridges to reach those who are not ready to step back into a sanctuary. By meeting young people where they already are on their phones, laptops, and social feeds we can extend an invitation that feels relevant and authentic.

Third, we can model a faith that is lived out, not just preached about. Younger generations are drawn to authenticity. They want to see faith in action injustice confronted, communities served, relationships restored. When we live what we say we believe, they notice.

And finally, we can pray not for their return to the way things were, but for a renewal of faith that meets the needs of today's world. Prayer is not a last resort; it is our first step toward understanding, connection, and healing.

The generational drift does not have to mean the end of the story. It is an opportunity to listen deeply, adapt humbly, and love relentlessly. The pews may be emptier today, but with open hearts and open minds, we can begin to draw them back not just to a building, but to a living faith that matters.

Chapter Three: Faith on the Clock

It is a phrase I hear all too often: "I just don't have time for church."

At first, it seemed like an excuse an easy out for those who might not be interested. But over the years, I have come to realize that for many, it is a painful truth. Our lives have become so packed with work, school, kids' activities, appointments, and endless to-do lists that even a Sunday morning feels like a luxury they cannot afford.

I have watched families rush in halfway through the service, juggling diaper bags and snacks, glancing at watches to see if they will make it to the next appointment. I have seen businesspeople take phone calls in the church lobby, and students flip through assignments on their phones between hymns. Even for those who genuinely want to be part of a faith community, the pull of life's demands often drowns out the gentle call to worship.

And for some, the thought of giving up a precious day off a day to rest, to catch up, to simply breathe feels overwhelming.

I remember visiting a young couple who used to attend faithfully but had recently stopped coming. They both worked long hours, barely saw each other during the week, and Sunday had become their only chance to reconnect as a family. They were not hostile to church they just felt they were barely surviving, and adding another obligation, even a spiritual one, felt impossible.

As I listened, I realized something important: the issue is not always commitment it is ability. People are not necessarily rejecting faith or fellowship; they are struggling to find space for it in a world that moves at breakneck speed.

So, what is the solution?

It starts with rethinking our expectations. Instead of demanding more time from already overwhelmed people, what if we offered flexibility? Shorter, more focused services. Multiple service times.

Online options for those who cannot physically attend. Small groups that meet at convenient times and locations.

We can also shift our culture from obligation to invitation. Rather than making people feel guilty for missing church, we can celebrate the times they do come, however rare they may be. We can express genuine gratitude for their presence and encourage them to find ways to stay connected during the week.

Next, we must help people see faith as a daily rhythm, not a weekly event. Instead of seeing Sunday as "church day," we can emphasize how to live out faith amid work, family, and daily pressures. Devotions on the go. Prayer at the kitchen table. Service projects woven into ordinary life.

And finally, we can pray for wisdom. Pray that God will show us how to balance busy schedules with spiritual nourishment. Pray for creativity in finding ways to connect. Pray that, even in the busyness, hearts will remain open to His presence.

Faith on the clock does not have to mean faith forgotten. It means we are called to be creative, compassionate, and courageous in meeting people where they are and showing them that even in the busiest lives, there's still room for God.

Chapter Four: The Church Hurt

For some, the empty pews are not a result of busyness or disinterest they are a wound. These are the people who once walked through the church doors with hope, looking for community, grace, and healing. But instead, they found judgment, hypocrisy, betrayal, or even abuse.

I have sat across the table from people whose eyes filled with tears as they shared stories of being shamed for asking questions, of being dismissed when they needed support, of being excluded because of their struggles or failures. Some were hurt by leaders who prioritized power over people. Others were pushed aside by cliques or ignored during times of crisis.

It is easy to think these stories are rare exceptions, but they are more common than we would like to admit. The wounds may be hidden, but they are real, and they are deep. And for many, the easiest way to stop the pain was simply to walk away.

I remember a middle-aged man who once led a vibrant Bible study but had not set foot in a church in years. "It wasn't God I lost faith in," he said quietly. "It was people." His story is not unique. The truth is, when trust is broken, when a place that should be safe becomes a source of pain, the journey back is hard.

So, what can we do? How can we begin to heal these hurts and rebuild trust?

First, we need to acknowledge the wounds. Pretending they do not exist or offering shallow apologies will not bring healing. We must listen with compassion and humility, creating safe spaces for people to share their stories without fear of dismissal or judgment.

Second, we need to repent and seek reconciliation. This means not just saying "I'm sorry," but actively working to repair broken relationships. It might mean reaching out to those we know were hurt, offering a listening ear, or asking for forgiveness.

Third, we need to change our culture. A healthy church is not one that is perfect it is one that is honest, humble, and centered on grace. We can prioritize transparency in leadership, provide accountability, and create environments where questions and struggles are welcomed, not shamed.

And most importantly, we must lean into God's healing power. While we cannot erase the past, we can trust that God is in the business of restoration. Through prayer, patience, and perseverance, we can help mend broken hearts and rebuild a community where everyone feels truly welcome.

The church hurt is real, but it does not have to be the final word. Healing is possible, one conversation, one apology, one act of grace at a time.

Chapter Five: Entertainment vs. Engagement

It was a Sunday morning in a church I was visiting when it hit me. The stage was bright, the band played like a concert, and the screen behind them flashed perfectly timed graphics. The production was seamless. Everything was polished. But as I looked around the room, I noticed something missing.

The congregation sat back in their seats, arms crossed or hands in their laps. The music washed over them like background noise. A few sang quietly, but most watched, almost as if they were at a show instead of a worship service. When the final chord rang out and the lights shifted to a sermon introduction, a few glanced at their watches.

It was not that the church had done anything "wrong." In fact, the service had clearly been planned with care. But somewhere along the way, something essential had been lost. The focus had shifted from engagement a participatory experience of worship and connection to entertainment, where the audience watched and the "performers" led.

This is not an isolated issue. Across the country, churches have embraced slick presentations, professional-quality bands, and dynamic speakers, all in an effort to attract and keep attendees. The intentions are often good. After all, in a culture saturated with high-quality media and constant stimulation, shouldn't the church strive to be just as engaging?

But here is the danger: when worship becomes a performance, it stops being worship. When sermons are crafted to please rather than challenge, the truth can become watered down. When the goal shifts from making disciples to filling seats, faith can become shallow and consumer driven.

I have spoken with longtime churchgoers who quietly admit they feel more like spectators than participants. "I love the music," one said, "but I am not sure I am really connecting with God. It is like I am watching someone else worship." Another confessed, "It's entertaining, but I leave feeling more inspired by the band than by the message."

This shift is not just about preferences it is about the heart of the church's mission. Jesus did not call us to be consumers of spiritual experiences; He called us to be disciples, actively participating in His work of redemption. The early church was not known for flashy performances it was known for genuine community, deep teaching, shared resources, and transformed lives.

So how did we get here? How did the church, in its desire to reach people, risk turning worship into a show?

Part of the answer lies in the cultural shift toward instant gratification and entertainment-based experiences. People today are accustomed to scrolling through social media, watching Netflix, or attending live concerts. Churches have understandably felt pressure to compete with these formats to keep people engaged.

But the church is not called to compete with the world it is called to be different. To offer something deeper, more enduring, more transformative.

So, what is the solution?

First, we must reclaim the heart of worship. This means moving beyond lights and sound to focus on the presence of God. Worship should invite participation not just through singing, but through prayer, Scripture reading, silence, and shared testimonies. Leaders can model this by creating space for reflection and by inviting the congregation to respond, rather than simply see.

Second, we can prioritize substance over style. Yes, excellence in music and presentation is valuable, but it should never overshadow the message. Sermons should be rooted deeply in Scripture and challenge listeners to apply truth to their lives. Worship music should point to God, not just stir emotions.

Third, we need to create opportunities for real connection. Instead of relying solely on large services, we can invest in smaller gatherings

Bible studies, prayer groups, service projects where people can engage with one another and with God on a deeper level. When relationships form, when stories are shared, when needs are met, church becomes more than a performance it becomes a family.

Fourth, we should equip the congregation to lead. Instead of a few "professionals" running the service while everyone else watches, we can empower lay leaders to share their gifts. Let the church be a place where everyone contributes, where talents are used not for applause, but for ministry.

I think of a small rural church I once visited where there was no band, no fancy screens, no polished production. Instead, an older man played piano with a shaky hand, a young woman led hymns, and several members stood to share testimonies of God's work in their lives. It was not flashy, but it was real. And the Spirit was present in a way I have not often felt in much larger, more polished churches.

Finally, we can pray for a renewed hunger for engagement. Pray that our congregations will move from passive observers to active participants in the work of God. Pray that we will be bold enough to step away from the pressure to entertain and return to the simple, powerful call to love God and love people.

Entertainment may fill seats temporarily, but engagement changes lives. And in the end, that is what we are called to be about.

Chapter Six: The Rise of "Spiritual but Not Religious"

I once met a young woman at a coffee shop, notebook open and earbuds in. When I struck up a conversation, I discovered she was deeply spiritual. She spoke of prayer, of finding peace in nature, and of wrestling with the big questions of life. Yet, when I asked where she attended church, she hesitated. "Oh, I don't do church," she said softly. "I'm spiritual, but not religious."

That phrase has become increasingly common, echoing across generations and communities. It signals a shift a quiet but profound movement away from traditional religious institutions toward a more personal, individualized approach to faith. People still believe in something bigger than themselves. They still pray. They still seek purpose and meaning. But they no longer see church as necessary or even helpful in that journey.

Why?

For some, the answer is found in past wounds. Church hurt, judgmental attitudes, or legalistic teachings have driven them away. For others, it is the perception that churches are out of touch, more focused on politics or tradition than on compassion and relevance. Still others see church as unnecessary because they can "connect with God" in their own way through meditation, online content, or time in nature.

But at its core, this movement often reflects a deeper longing: for authenticity, connection, and a faith that feels real. Many of those who identify as "spiritual but not religious" are not rejecting God they are rejecting structures and systems that feel rigid, exclusionary, or performative.

I remember sitting with a man who had stopped attending church years ago. He told me, "I believe in God, but I do not need a middleman. I can pray on my own. Church just felt like a show." His words echoed a sentiment I have heard from many others: faith has become something personal, private, even hidden.

So, what can the church do in response? How do we speak to the hearts of those who still seek God but have given up on organized religion?

First, we must listen without defensiveness. When someone says they are "spiritual but not religious," it is easy to react with frustration or dismissiveness. But if we truly listen, we may hear stories of disappointment, disillusionment, or unmet needs. By honoring their experiences, we open the door to understanding and reconciliation.

Second, we need to embrace authenticity. Many have left the church because they perceived a gap between what was preached and what was practiced. They long for a faith that is honest about struggles, transparent about failures, and humble in its approach. Churches that foster genuine relationships and avoid pretenses will resonate with those looking for a more authentic spiritual experience.

Third, we can create spaces for spiritual exploration. Not everyone is ready to jump into formal membership or structured worship. What if we offered "spiritual conversations" in neutral spaces coffee shops, parks, online forums where questions and doubts are welcomed without judgment? These gatherings could focus on listening, sharing, and learning, rather than preaching or persuading.

Fourth, we must shift from institution to relationship. For those disillusioned with church structures, relationships are the key. Personal connections whether through a neighbor, a co-worker, or a family member can become bridges back to faith communities. Rather than inviting someone to a building, we can invite them into our lives. Shared meals, acts of service, and honest conversations can do more to rekindle faith than any formal program.

Fifth, we can reimagine what "church" means. The early church met in homes, shared meals, and cared for one another's needs. They did not have elaborate structures or programs they had community. Today, we can recapture that spirit by focusing less on Sunday services and more on cultivating relationships that reflect Christ's love. Home groups, service projects, and neighborhood gatherings can become expressions of church that feel accessible and authentic.

Finally, we must pray for a revival of genuine faith. Pray that God will draw hearts back not to buildings or programs, but to Him. Pray that those who are spiritual but not religious will meet the living Christ through acts of love, words of truth, and relationships marked by grace.

I think back to the young woman at the coffee shop. I did not invite her to my church. I invited her to lunch. We shared stories, talked about faith, and found common ground. Over time, she began to ask more questions, and eventually, she found her way into a small group where she felt safe to explore her faith further.

The rise of "spiritual but not religious" does not have to signal the decline of faith. It is a challenge and an opportunity for the church to return to its roots: authentic relationships, humble service, and unwavering love.

Chapter Seven: Pastor Burnout and Pulpit Fatigue

When people talk about the challenges facing the church today, they often focus on declining attendance, shifting cultural values, or financial pressures. But behind many of these struggles lies another, quieter crisis: the exhaustion of pastors and church leaders.

I remember sitting with a friend, a pastor who had faithfully served his congregation for over twenty years. His shoulders slumped, his voice was quiet, and his eyes were tired. "I feel like I'm running on fumes," he admitted. "I am giving everything I have, but it is never enough. There is always more to do, more people to reach, more fires to put out. And I do not know how much longer I can keep this up."

His story is not unique. Across the country, pastors are facing increasing demands with diminishing resources. They are expected to be preachers, counselors, administrators, fundraisers, visionaries, and crisis managers all while keeping their own spiritual health and family life. The weight of expectations is heavy, and many feel isolated, undervalued, and overwhelmed.

Studies show that a significant percentage of pastors have considered leaving ministry, not because they have lost their faith, but because they are exhausted. They are tired of navigating conflict, of trying to meet impossible expectations, of pouring themselves out with little rest or replenishment. Some have faced betrayal from those they trusted. Others have carried the burden of congregational decline, feeling as though every empty pew is a personal failure.

Pulpit fatigue is not just about physical tiredness it is about emotional and spiritual depletion. When pastors feel they must constantly perform, when their worth is tied to numbers and outcomes, when they have no safe space to be vulnerable, burnout becomes inevitable.

So, what is the solution? How can we as congregations and as a wider church community care for our leaders and prevent burnout?

First, we must normalize sabbath and rest. Pastors need regular time away from the demands of ministry not just vacations, but intentional sabbath rest. Congregations can encourage this by providing sabbaticals, respecting days off, and not expecting constant availability. A rested pastor is a more effective, more compassionate leader.

Second, we need to create support systems. Isolation is one of the greatest threats to pastoral health. Churches can form care teams or accountability groups where pastors can share struggles without fear of judgment. Denominations and associations can provide retreats, counseling services, and mentorship programs. No pastor should feel they have to carry the load alone.

Third, we can adjust expectations. Instead of measuring a pastor's worth by attendance numbers, budgets, or programs, we can value faithfulness, integrity, and spiritual depth. We can shift from a consumer mindset where the pastor "delivers," and the congregation "consumes" to a collaborative model where everyone shares in the work of ministry.

Fourth, congregations can practice gratitude and encouragement. A simple word of thanks, a handwritten note, or a public acknowledgment of a pastor's service can make a world of difference. Letting leaders know they are appreciated and seen can lift heavy hearts and renew weary spirits.

Fifth, we can equip lay leaders to share the load. Many pastors feel burned out because they are doing work that could and should be shared. By training and empowering members to lead ministries, care for others, and make decisions, we free pastors to focus on their unique calling. This creates a healthier, more sustainable church culture.

Finally, we must pray for our pastors. Pray for their strength, wisdom, and protection. Pray that God will renew their passion and deepen their faith. Pray that they will find rest in His presence and joy in their calling.

I think of Jesus, who often withdrew to solitary places to pray, even during pressing needs. His example reminds us that ministry is not a sprint it is a marathon. It requires rhythms of work and rest, giving and receiving, leading, and following.

Pastor burnout and pulpit fatigue are real, but they are not inevitable. With intentional care, shared responsibility, and a commitment to holistic health, we can create environments where pastors thrive and congregations flourish.

Because when the shepherd is healthy, the flock is more likely to thrive.

Chapter Eight: The Digital Dilemma

It was only a few years ago when churches, especially small ones, debated the necessity of streaming services or posting sermons online. Many worried that offering digital options might discourage physical attendance. But then, almost overnight, the world changed. The COVID-19 pandemic shut church doors, scattered congregations, and forced pastors and leaders to pivot, learning overnight how to livestream worship, host Zoom Bible studies, and keep connection through screens.

For many churches, the digital shift was a lifeline. It kept congregations connected during isolation. It provided access for vulnerable members. It even expanded reach beyond traditional boundaries, drawing in viewers from other towns, states, and even countries.

Yet now, even as physical gatherings have resumed, the digital dilemma is still. Some churches have embraced online ministry as a permanent feature. Others have struggled with reduced in-person attendance, as members opt for the convenience of online worship. Still others face budgetary strain trying to keep technology upgrades while rekindling in-person engagement.

And it is not just the mechanics of live streaming it is the deeper question of what church really is. Is a streamed service enough? Can true community form through screens? Can digital worship replace the gathered body of Christ?

I have heard pastors wrestle with these questions. Some see online services as a tool for outreach, a way to meet people where they are. Others worry that it fosters passivity, creating "armchair Christians" who consume content but remain disconnected from the life of the church.

A young woman I spoke with put it bluntly: "I love watching my church service online in my pajamas. It is easy. But I know deep down it is different from being there. I just cannot seem to get myself to go back in person." Her words capture the tension. Technology offers convenience, but it also tempts us to settle for less.

So, what is the solution? How can the church embrace the benefits of digital tools without losing the heart of embodied, communal faith?

First, we must redefine the purpose of digital ministry. It is not a replacement for physical gathering it is a bridge. Online services can connect with those who are curious, cautious, or unable to attend in person. They can provide a first step toward deeper involvement. But we must consistently communicate that church is more than content it is community. The goal is not to keep people online forever but to invite them into relationships where they can grow and serve.

Second, we can prioritize engagement over consumption. Many online services are designed for passive viewing. What if we shifted the model to invite interaction? Chat features, live prayer rooms, virtual discussion groups, and follow-up calls can turn viewers into participants. When people feel seen and valued, they are more likely to stay connected and move toward deeper involvement.

Third, we need to offer hybrid opportunities. Some will always need digital options due to health, distance, or circumstances. By offering hybrid gatherings where online participants are acknowledged and included alongside in-person attendees we model inclusivity and flexibility. Small groups can meet both online and offline. Classes can be recorded for those who cannot attend. Leadership meetings can include remote participation.

Fourth, we must teach digital discernment. The internet offers a vast array of spiritual content—some helpful, some misleading, some outright harmful. Churches can provide resources and guidance to help members navigate this landscape. By recommending trustworthy podcasts, YouTube channels, and online study tools, we equip people to grow in faith even as they engage with digital media.

Fifth, we can model embodied faith. Even as we use digital tools, we must emphasize the importance of real-world presence. Acts of service, communal meals, baptisms, weddings, funerals these are moments that cannot be fully replicated online. We can remind our congregations that faith is lived out in bodies, in shared spaces, in physical acts of love and service.

I remember a family who joined our church online during the pandemic. For months, they attended virtually, grateful for the connection. But when we finally reopened, they hesitated. The kids were nervous about meeting new friends. The parents were unsure if they would feel welcome. So, we reached out. We sent personal notes, made phone calls, and invited them to a small outdoor gathering. When they finally came in person, they were greeted with warmth and recognized from their online participation. Over time, they found a home not just on the livestream, but in the pews, in the potlucks, and in the service projects.

Sixth, we must pray for wisdom in this digital age. Technology is a powerful tool, but it cannot replace the transforming work of the Spirit. Pray that God will guide us in using digital media to extend His love, without losing sight of the embodied nature of the church. Pray that we will resist the temptation to measure success by views or likes and instead focus on lives changed and communities transformed.

And finally, we need to be patient. The digital shift will not resolve overnight. Some will return to in-person gatherings quickly; others may need time and encouragement. Some may never return but can still be connected in meaningful ways. As we navigate this new landscape, let us extend grace to our leaders, to our members, and to ourselves.

The digital dilemma is not just a challenge it is an opportunity. An opportunity to reach further, connect deeper, and remind a scattered, busy, online world that true community is possible, and it begins with love.

Chapter Nine: Faith in a Post-Pandemic World

There was a moment, sometime in mid-2020, when the entire world seemed to hold its breath. Churches closed their doors. Services were canceled. Fellowship halls stood silent. The usual rhythms of Sunday worship, midweek Bible studies, choir rehearsals, and potluck dinners all came to an abrupt halt. It was not just our routines that were disrupted; it was our sense of connection, our experience of shared faith, our understanding of what it meant to be the church.

For months, congregations scrambled to adapt. Pastors preached into cameras in empty sanctuaries. Worship teams recorded songs from their living rooms. Communion became something you shared with crackers and juice at your kitchen table. For many, this was a lifeline. It kept faith alive when fear and uncertainty gripped the world.

But now, as the pandemic has receded and restrictions have eased, a new question has appeared: What does faith look like in a post-pandemic world? Will we simply return to the old patterns, pretending nothing happened? Or will we learn from what we experienced the grief, the resilience, the isolation, and the creativity to forge a new path forward?

The truth is that the pandemic changed us. It exposed both the strengths and the weaknesses of our churches. It revealed our ability for adaptability, but it also laid bare how much we depended on Sunday gatherings as the primary expression of faith. It reminded us that the church is not a building or a program it is the people, the body of Christ, called to love and serve in every season.

I have spoken with countless pastors and congregants in the aftermath of those long, uncertain months. Some have been eager to return to in-person worship, craving the tangible connection of shared space. Others are still hesitant, whether due to health concerns, lingering habits, or spiritual disconnection. Some have simply disappeared, their absence as sudden as it is silent.

One pastor told me, "I used to think if we opened the doors, people would come back. But now I realize that reopening is just the beginning. We need to rebuild trust, reconnect relationships, and reimagine what it means to be the church." His words resonated deeply.

So, how do we move forward? How do we cultivate faith in a post-pandemic world where old assumptions no longer hold, and new challenges demand new responses?

First, we must acknowledge the grief. The pandemic left a mark on all of us. We lost loved ones, jobs, security, and even some of our faith communities. Churches should create spaces to lament and heal through memorial services, prayer vigils, and small group conversations where stories can be shared and burdens lifted. Healing comes when we name the losses and invite God into our pain.

Second, we can embrace hybrid church models. The pandemic taught us that while physical gathering is essential, digital tools can complement and extend our reach. Online services, virtual Bible studies, and social media engagement should not replace in-person fellowship but can serve as bridges for those who cannot yet return or for new people exploring faith from a distance. A blended approach honors both connection and accessibility.

Third, we need to rebuild relationships intentionally. Isolation fractured communities. People grew disconnected, and the longer they stayed away, the harder it became to return. Churches can respond by launching "Reconnect" initiatives phone calls, personal visits, neighborhood gatherings where members check in with one another, listen without judgment, and offer invitations to re-engage. This is not about guilt-tripping or shaming; it is about reweaving the fabric of community.

Fourth, we can simplify and refocus. Many churches found during the pandemic that programs and activities once thought essential were, in fact, distractions from the core mission. This is a chance to streamline, focusing on worship, discipleship, service, and community. Instead of rushing back into busy schedules, we can ask: What truly matters? What reflects the heart of Christ?

Fifth, we can foster resilience. The pandemic will not be the last crisis we face. Churches that survived and even thrived during the shutdowns did so by cultivating adaptability, collaboration, and deep-rooted faith. We can build on these lessons, equipping congregations to respond to future challenges with courage and creativity. Resilient faith is not afraid of change; it leans into it with hope.

Sixth, we must prioritize mental and spiritual health. The pandemic left many struggling with anxiety, depression, and spiritual fatigue. Churches can offer counseling resources, prayer ministries, and honest conversations about mental health. Leaders should model vulnerability, acknowledge their own struggles, and encourage others to seek help. A healthy church is one that cares for the whole person body, mind, and spirit.

I remember a woman who shared with me how deeply her faith was shaken during the pandemic. She felt isolated, anxious, and disconnected from her church community. But what helped her was not a livestream or a sermon it was a simple phone call from a church member who listened, prayed with her, and reminded her she was not alone. That call rekindled her hope and her desire to reconnect with her faith community.

Seventh, we need to recommit to mission. The pandemic highlighted the deep needs in our communities' hunger, poverty, loneliness, injustice. Churches have a renewed opportunity to be the hands and feet of Jesus, serving not just those inside the walls but those outside. Food drives, mental health support, tutoring programs, and justice initiatives can be practical expressions of the Gospel in a hurting world.

Finally, we must pray. Pray for wisdom to navigate this new landscape. Pray for courage to change what needs changing. Pray for compassion to reach those who are lost or struggling. Pray for revival not just of numbers, but of hearts ignited by the love of Christ.

The post-pandemic world is uncharted territory. It is easy to feel overwhelmed or uncertain. But it is also a profound opportunity a chance to rediscover the essence of church, to build deeper relationships, to serve with renewed passion, and to trust that God is still at work, even in the midst of disruption.

Faith in a post-pandemic world will not look exactly like it did before. And that is okay. Because the church is not called to preserve the past it is called to follow Jesus into the future.

Chapter Ten: Doctrine Wars and Denominational Division

In the quiet corners of churches, over coffee in fellowship halls, and across digital platforms, debates have simmered and sometimes boiled over questions of doctrine. Long-held beliefs and interpretations, once considered settled, have become flashpoints. Denominations have splintered, congregations have split, and friendships have been strained. It is a painful reality of modern church life: while the world outside drifts further from organized religion, inside the church walls, many are entangled in battles over theology, practice, and cultural issues.

I have witnessed the damage firsthand. A congregation I once knew was torn apart over differing interpretations of Scripture related to human sexuality. Once-vibrant ministries faltered, attendance plummeted, and even long-standing friendships were shattered. In another church, intense arguments over worship styles and leadership decisions led to an exodus of families who had once been pillars of the community.

Why does this happen? Why do doctrinal disagreements, often rooted in deeply held convictions, lead to such division?

Part of the answer lies in the human tendency to equate faithfulness with certainty. When we become convinced that our understanding of Scripture is the only correct one, we can easily dismiss, judge, or even condemn those who see things differently. This attitude, though often born from a desire to uphold truth, can harden hearts and create an environment where grace is overshadowed by rigidity.

Another factor is the way cultural issues have intersected with church life. Topics like gender roles, racial justice, LGBTQ+ inclusion, and political affiliations have stirred deep emotions and sparked controversy. For some, these debates feel like tests of orthodoxy. For others, they represent an opportunity to extend compassion and inclusivity. The tension between these perspectives has left many churches fractured and fatigued.

I recall a conversation with a pastor who confided, "I feel like I am walking a tightrope. No matter what I say or do not say someone will be upset. It is exhausting." His weariness echoed the struggles of countless leaders trying to shepherd diverse congregations with integrity and sensitivity.

Yet, amidst the division, I have also seen glimmers of hope. I have met congregations that, despite differences in belief, have chosen to focus on what unites them: a shared love for Christ, a commitment to serving their community, and a willingness to listen with humility. These churches have discovered that unity does not require uniformity, and that love is a stronger bond than agreement on every point of doctrine.

So, what can we do to move beyond doctrine wars and denominational division? How can the church model a separate way of being a way marked by grace, humility, and a commitment to the Gospel more than anything else?

First, we must prioritize relationship over being right. While doctrine matters and truth is essential, our relationships with one another are a living testimony of the Gospel. Jesus said the world would know we are His disciples by our love for one another, not our theological precision. This does not mean we abandon truth, but that we approach disagreements with a posture of humility and love.

Second, we can create spaces for honest dialogue. Rather than avoiding controversial topics, churches can host forums, Bible studies, or listening sessions where differing perspectives are shared and heard. When people feel safe to express their thoughts without fear of judgment, understanding can grow. Leaders can model respectful conversation, acknowledge complexity, and avoid oversimplification.

Third, we should focus on core doctrines. Many divisions arise over secondary issues, while core beliefs like the divinity of Christ, the resurrection, and salvation by grace are shared. By emphasizing these essentials, we can remind ourselves of the common ground we stand on, even amidst differing interpretations on other matters.

Fourth, we need to practice confession and forgiveness. Division often leaves wounds words spoken in anger, relationships broken by pride, communities fractured by bitterness. Healing begins with repentance and extends through forgiveness. Churches can create moments for public confession and reconciliation, inviting God's Spirit to mend what has been broken.

Fifth, we must remember the mission. The church's purpose is not to win theological arguments or outdo other denominations. It is to make disciples, love neighbors, and bear witness to the kingdom of God. When our focus shifts from internal battles to external mission, unity becomes not just possible but necessary.

I remember a small-town church that had been divided for years over worship styles. Traditionalists sat on one side of the sanctuary: contemporary worshipers on the other. One day, after a series of prayer meetings and honest conversations, the congregation decided to blend their services not to please everyone, but to reflect their unity in Christ. It was not perfect, and not everyone was happy. But something shifted. Walls came down. People began to see one another not as opponents but as family.

Sixth, we can embrace denominational diversity as a strength. Instead of viewing other churches or denominations as competitors or threats, we can celebrate the richness of God's kingdom expressed through diverse traditions. Joint community projects, shared worship events, and collaborative service efforts can show that while we may differ in practice, we are united in purpose.

Seventh, we must pray. Pray for softened hearts, for wisdom in leadership, and for a spirit of unity that transcends human differences. Pray that God will heal wounds, restore relationships, and remind us that the church is His, not ours.

In a world increasingly marked by division political, social, cultural the church has an opportunity to model something different. To show that love can bridge differences, that grace can triumph over judgment, and that unity does not require uniformity.

Doctrine matters. Truth matters. But love matters most.

Chapter Eleven: Community Without a Sanctuary

I once visited a small congregation that had lost its church building to a fire. For years, that building had been the center of their faith community the place where generations had worshiped, where couples had married, where babies had been dedicated, and where saints had been laid to rest. When the fire reduced the sanctuary to rubble, it was not just a structure that was lost it was a piece of their identity.

But what struck me was not their despair. It was their resilience. Within days, they gathered in a local community center. Folding chairs replaced pews. A borrowed piano substituted for the pipe organ. The familiar stained glass was gone, replaced by bare walls and folding tables. Yet as they sang hymns and shared testimonies, I saw something powerful. Their community had not been destroyed by the loss of their sanctuary it had been redefined.

Across the country, many churches are discovering a similar truth, though not always by fire. Rising costs, aging buildings, declining attendance, and even shifting priorities have led some congregations to close their sanctuaries or sell their properties. Others have found themselves displaced by circumstances beyond their control. And still others have realized that ministry does not have to be confined to a specific place.

This shift challenges our assumptions. For generations, we have equated "church" with a building a steeple on a hill, a set of pews, a pulpit, and a fellowship hall. But the early church did not have these things. They met in homes, gathered in public spaces, shared meals, and lived their faith in the everyday rhythms of life.

I have spoken with members of congregations that no longer have a physical sanctuary. Some describe the first loss as heartbreaking, even disorienting. But over time, many have found that being "homeless" forced them to focus on what truly matters: the people, not the place.

One small church I visited holds Sunday worship in a park when the weather is good. They spread blankets, set up a portable speaker, and invite anyone passing by to join. On rainy days, they gather in a local coffee shop or community center. They do not have a steeple, but they have a spirit of welcome and inclusion that draws people in.

Another church turned its closure into an opportunity. When they realized their dwindling membership could no longer sustain the upkeep of their aging building, they sold it and used the funds to support mission work and community outreach. They now meet in homes and public spaces, focusing their energy on serving others rather than supporting property.

These stories inspire me, but they also challenge me. What does it mean to be a faith community without a sanctuary? How do we keep a sense of identity, belonging, and purpose when we do not have a "home base"?

Here are some practical solutions:

First, we must embrace the idea that church is not a place it is a people. The Bible never defines the church as a building. It describes it as a body, a family, a living organism. When we lose sight of this, we risk tying our faith too closely to walls and structures. By re-centering on relationships and shared mission, we can keep community even without a dedicated space.

Second, we can focus on flexible, creative gathering spaces. Parks, libraries, homes, coffee shops, rented halls all can become sanctuaries when filled with worship, prayer, and fellowship. The key is to keep consistency and clarity about where and when gatherings happen, so people feel connected and included.

Third, we can use technology to stay connected. Digital tools like group chats, livestreams, online prayer meetings, and social media updates help keep a sense of community even when physical gathering is limited. This is especially important for members who may be homebound, traveling, or hesitant to attend in person.

Fourth, we should strengthen personal connections. Without a central building, relationships become even more vital. Leaders can organize regular check-ins, prayer partners, and small group gatherings to keep people engaged and supported. Sharing meals, celebrating milestones, and walking through challenges together reinforces the sense of belonging.

Fifth, we can turn outward in mission. Without the expenses and distractions of building maintenance, a church can redirect its resources and energy toward serving the broader community. Food pantries, tutoring programs, neighborhood cleanups, and partnerships with local organizations can become the new "sanctuary," where God's love is shown in action.

I think of a church that lost its building due to financial constraints but decided to "adopt" a local elementary school. They provided backpacks, school supplies, after-school tutoring, and support for families in need. The congregation may not have a building with their name on it, but they have become known as the church that shows up for the community.

Sixth, we need to nurture a strong shared identity. Even without a physical sanctuary, a faith community can create a sense of identity through shared values, consistent communication, and intentional discipleship. This might include a common mission statement, regular teaching themes, and clear opportunities for involvement.

Finally, we must pray. Pray for wisdom, creativity, and courage. Pray that the Spirit will bind us together in unity and purpose, even when we are scattered. Pray that we will see our "sanctuary" not as a building, but as the space where God's people gather whether under a roof, in a park, or across digital platforms.

The absence of a sanctuary does not mean the absence of God's presence. In fact, it may just remind us that He is not confined to any one place. He is with us wherever we gather in His name.

When the pews grow empty and the sanctuary is gone, the church is not dead. It is alive in every handshake, every shared meal, every act of service, every whispered prayer. Because the church is not a place. It is us.

Chapter Twelve: The Missing Men

I have sat in countless Sunday morning services, scanning the sanctuary with a familiar pang of awareness. Women, children, and elderly men often fill the pews, but younger and middle-aged men are conspicuously absent. In Bible studies, prayer groups, and volunteer rosters, the imbalance is just as clear. Where are the men?

This is not merely a local issue it is a pattern seen across many congregations. In some churches, men make up less than 40% of the active membership. In others, especially in mainline denominations, that number dips even lower. While many factors contribute to church decline, the absence of men and especially young and middle-aged men has become one of the most noticeable trends in recent decades.

So, what is behind this missing presence?

Part of the answer lies in cultural shifts. For generations, the church was a central institution in many communities. Men were expected to take part, lead, and pass down faith traditions to their families. But as societal roles have changed, so too has the perception of church. Many men today view faith communities as irrelevant, feminized, or disconnected from their personal and professional lives.

Some men struggle with the relational focus of church. Services often emphasize sharing emotions, talking about feelings, or engaging in activities that may feel uncomfortable or unfamiliar. For men shaped by a culture that prizes stoicism, competition, and independence, church can seem like a place where they do not fit.

Others have been alienated by church messaging. Sermons that emphasize weakness, brokenness, or surrender can feel dissonant with a man's desire to be strong, competent, and in control. While humility and vulnerability are key aspects of Christian discipleship, they must be framed in ways that resonate with a masculine journey toward purpose, leadership, and resilience.

Then there are the men who have simply fallen away from faith altogether. Maybe they were raised in church but found it boring, irrelevant, or judgmental. Maybe they drifted during college or early adulthood and never returned. Or perhaps life's pressures career demands, family responsibilities, financial stress have crowded out time for worship and fellowship.

I recall a conversation with a man in his forties who said, "Church feels like it is for women and kids. I do not see where I fit in." His words were not spoken in anger, but in quiet resignation. He did not feel hostility toward faith; he just felt disconnected.

But here is the truth: the church needs men. Not because they are better or more important, but because God's kingdom is incomplete without them. Men bring unique strengths leadership, service, creativity, mentorship that can bless the church and the wider community.

So how do we bring them back? How do we re-engage men who have drifted away, who feel marginalized, or who have never felt at home in the church?

Here are some practical solutions:

First, we must reframe church as a place of purpose and challenge. Many men are drawn to challenges that require courage, resilience, and action. Sermons and ministries that emphasize mission, justice, and service can resonate deeply. Instead of portraying faith as passive or sentimental, we can highlight its call to radical discipleship, sacrificial love, and courageous living.

Second, we can create spaces for men to connect authentically. Men's groups that go beyond breakfast meetings and Bible studies offering hands-on service projects, outdoor adventures, or mentoring programs can provide environments where men feel comfortable sharing their lives and growing in faith. These spaces should be marked by trust, respect, and mutual encouragement.

Third, we need to model male leadership and mentorship. When younger men see older men serving faithfully, leading with integrity, and balancing strength with humility, they are more likely to engage. Churches can intentionally pair younger and older men in mentorship relationships, providing opportunities for wisdom to be passed down and for younger men to grow in confidence.

Fourth, we can address practical barriers. Many men face work schedules, family obligations, and fatigue that make regular church attendance difficult. Churches can offer flexible gathering times, online resources, and family-friendly environments that acknowledge and accommodate these realities.

Fifth, we must offer grace and patience. Some men have deep wounds from past church experiences, from struggles with addiction, from broken relationships that keep them away. We can respond not with condemnation but with understanding and compassion. Listening to their stories, acknowledging their pain, and offering a path forward marked by grace can open the door to healing.

I think of a church that started a Saturday morning men's group that combined community service with fellowship. They built wheelchair ramps for seniors, repaired homes for single mothers, and shared meals afterward. Over time, men who had been absent from Sunday services found belonging and purpose in these gatherings. Some eventually returned to worship, drawn not by obligation but by a sense of shared mission.

Sixth, we can pray intentionally for men. Pray for their hearts to be softened, for their identities to be rooted in Christ, for their roles as fathers, husbands, brothers, and sons to be strengthened. Pray that they will see the church not as a place of obligation, but as a community where they are needed and valued.

Finally, we must remember that men, like everyone else, are drawn to authentic love. When churches become places where people are truly seen, heard, and valued, hearts begin to open. Men need not be convinced with clever programs or guilt-laden sermons they need to meet the love of Christ through relationships that challenge and inspire.

The missing men are not a lost cause. They are a calling a reminder that the church must be a place where everyone, regardless of gender or background, can find belonging and purpose. It is not about making church "manly" or pandering to stereotypes. It is about creating space for men to meet God in ways that are real, relevant, and transformative.

The pews may be emptier today, but with intentional effort, compassionate outreach, and a renewed focus on authentic community, those seats can be filled again not just with bodies, but with men whose lives are ignited by the Gospel and committed to building the kingdom of God.

Chapter Thirteen: Worship Wars

It begins innocently enough. One Sunday, the congregation sings a new worship song upbeat, with drums and electric guitars. Some clap along; others fold their arms, frowning. The next week, the familiar hymns are absent, replaced by a modern praise set. A few long timers quietly leave before the closing prayer. Over coffee in the fellowship hall, murmurs of dissatisfaction ripple through the room.

What starts as a simple shift in musical style can soon escalate into deep division: the so-called "worship wars." It is a conflict that has divided congregations, strained relationships, and even caused church splits. At its heart lies a question far more profound than music preference: What is worship really about?

For generations, traditional hymns with pipe organs, choirs, and structured liturgy defined the worship experience. These songs carried theological depth, poetic beauty, and a sense of reverence. But as churches looked to reach younger generations, many embraced contemporary styles worship bands, praise choruses, informal liturgies. For some, this brought vitality and connection. For others, it felt like abandoning heritage and sacredness.

I remember visiting a church where the worship leader opened the service with a fast, modern praise song. The band played with passion; the words projected on large screens. A group near the front raised their hands; others in the back remained silent, shifting uncomfortably. After the service, an older member approached me and said, "I miss the hymns. It does not feel like church anymore." A younger member overheard and replied, "But this is what connects with me. Should not church meet us where we are?"

Their exchange captured the heart of the worship wars. It is not just about music it is about identity, belonging, and how we approach God. For some, hymns connect them to generations past, anchoring their faith in tradition. For others, contemporary songs reflect their daily language and emotions, helping them engage authentically.

So how do we navigate these tensions? How do we move beyond the battleground of preference and discover a worship that unites rather than divides?

First, we must remember the purpose of worship. Worship is not about pleasing personal tastes or preferences. It is about glorifying God lifting our hearts in adoration, surrender, and gratitude. Whether through ancient hymns or modern choruses, worship is an offering to the One who created us. When we make worship about us our style, our comfort, our nostalgia we risk missing the point entirely.

I think of the Psalms, where David writes, "Sing to the Lord a new song" (Psalm 96:1) and also commands, "Remember the works of old" (Psalm 77:11). Worship has always included both remembering and renewing honoring tradition while embracing new expressions.

Second, we need to foster empathy and understanding. In many worship conflicts, the lines are drawn by age. Older members feel alienated by new styles; younger members feel constrained by traditions. Instead of judging one another, we can invite conversations. Listening sessions, where people share what certain songs mean to them, can build bridges. When an older member explains how a hymn sustained them through grief, or a younger member shares how a praise song speaks to their struggles, hearts begin to soften.

I recall a church that hosted a "Worship Stories" night. Members of all ages shared testimonies about a song that deeply affected their faith. As stories were told, the room filled with tears, laughter, and a new understanding. Suddenly, hymns and contemporary songs were not just styles they were vessels of faith.

Third, we can embrace blended worship. Churches do not have to choose between traditional and contemporary they can honor both. A service that includes a hymn followed by a modern song, or a traditional reading paired with a contemporary prayer, models unity in diversity.

This approach signals that all expressions of worship are valued and that the church is a place where everyone belongs.

One church I visited began each service with a hymn, moved into a contemporary praise set, and closed with a simple, a cappella chorus. Over time, congregants of different generations found themselves singing along with one another, discovering shared ground in worshiping God.

Fourth, we can focus on theological depth. The style of music matters less than the substance of the message. Whether a hymn or a modern song, worship should be grounded in Scripture and theology. Churches can evaluate song choices not by tempo or instrumentation but by the truth they convey. A powerful, biblically sound contemporary song can be just as reverent as a centuries-old hymn.

Fifth, we can engage congregants in the planning process. Worship planning often happens behind closed doors, leading to decisions that feel top-down. Inviting members from different age groups and backgrounds to help plan services fosters ownership and reduces resistance. When people feel heard and involved, they are more likely to embrace changes.

Sixth, we can teach about worship's purpose and history. Many conflicts arise from misunderstandings. Sermon series, workshops, or classes on the theology of worship can help congregants appreciate the richness of different traditions. Learning about the origins of beloved hymns or the biblical foundation of contemporary worship can foster respect and curiosity.

I once heard a worship leader share the story behind "It Is Well with My Soul." As he described Horatio Spafford's profound loss and unwavering faith, the congregation young and old was visibly moved. When they sang the hymn that morning, it was not just an old song; it was a shared declaration of trust in God.

Seventh, we must model humility and flexibility. Leaders' pastors, worship directors, musicians set the tone. When they approach worship with humility, acknowledging different preferences while staying focused on Christ, the congregation follows. When leaders are willing to adapt, to try new things, and to prioritize unity over personal preference, the church becomes a place of peace rather than conflict.

One pastor I know rotates worship styles throughout the year some weeks lean traditional, others contemporary, and others blended. He reminds the congregation that while we may not love every song, we are called to worship together as a family. Over time, this approach has built a resilient, gracious congregation.

Eighth, we can pray for unity. The enemy delights in division, especially over something as central as worship. Prayer is a powerful weapon against disunity. Praying for softened hearts, for mutual respect, and for a shared focus on God's glory can break down walls and heal wounds.

Finally, we can remember that worship is about surrender. Whether we sing from a hymnal or a screen, whether accompanied by an organ or a guitar, worship is an act of laying down our pride, preferences, and distractions to focus on God. It is not about the style it is about the heart.

The worship wars do not have to define us. With humility, empathy, creativity, and a shared commitment to glorifying God, we can move beyond division and discover a worship that unites, uplifts, and transforms.

Because in the end, worship is not a battle to be won. It is a gift to be shared.

Chapter Fourteen: The Church of Me

It is an idea that creeps in subtly, often unnoticed: the notion that church exists to meet my needs, to cater to my preferences, and to serve my desires. Over time, this mindset has quietly reshaped many congregations, shifting the focus from Christ-centered worship and community to something more consumer-driven something that resembles a spiritual marketplace rather than a sacred family.

I have seen it happen in small ways. Someone leaves a church because the sermons did not "feed them," or the music was not "their style." Another moves on because a ministry they liked was discontinued, or because the building did not have enough parking. Some skip worship entirely when life gets busy, rationalizing that "I can connect with God on my own."

These are not isolated attitudes they reflect a broader cultural shift. We live in a world where personal choice is king. Streaming services offer endless customization; restaurants craft menus to individual tastes; social media algorithms curate content to our preferences. It is easy to carry this mindset into our spiritual lives, expecting the church to adapt to us rather than the other way around.

The problem with the "Church of Me" is that it subtly replaces the Gospel's call to self-denial with a pursuit of self-satisfaction. Instead of asking, how can I serve? we ask, how can this church serve me? Instead of Where is God calling me? we ask, what is most convenient?

I remember a young couple who joined a church because of its dynamic children's program. As soon as their kids grew older and aged out of the program, they quietly left, looking for another church with "better offerings." Their faith community had become a commodity, something to be consumed rather than committed to.

Another man told me he stopped attending church during the pandemic because he discovered he could watch services online while sipping coffee in his pajamas. "It's easier this way," he said. "I still get the message, but I don't have to deal with the hassle of people or schedules."

While online access is a valuable tool especially for those with mobility challenges or health concerns it can also feed into the notion that church is about convenience, comfort, and personal preference.

But the biblical vision of church is far different. The early church was not built on consumerism it was built on commitment. In Acts 2, we read that the believers devoted themselves to the apostles' teaching, to fellowship, to the breaking of bread, and to prayer. They shared everything they had, cared for one another's needs, and worshiped together with glad and sincere hearts. Their focus was not on what they could get, but on whom they could serve.

So how do we counter the pull of the Church of Me? How do we reorient our hearts and our communities toward the self-giving love modeled by Christ?

Here are some expanded, practical solutions:

First, we can teach and model a theology of commitment. Commitment is a countercultural value in a world obsessed with personal choice. Preaching and teaching can highlight the importance of sticking with a community, even when it is imperfect. Leaders and long-time members can share their own stories of perseverance through conflict, disappointment, or change. Commitment to a local church mirrors God's covenant commitment to us.

Second, we can shift the focus from programs to people. Programs are valuable tools, but they should never replace the core mission of building relationships and making disciples. Instead of measuring success by attendance at events or the number of programs offered, we can focus on the depth of connection, the authenticity of relationships, and the fruit of spiritual growth.

I remember a church that canceled its large annual conference and redirected the funds to support small groups and one-on-one mentoring.

Over time, they saw deeper spiritual engagement and stronger relational bonds.

Third, we can encourage servant-hearted participation. Instead of asking, what can this church offer me, we can ask, where can I serve? This might mean volunteering in children's ministry, joining a prayer team, serving in community outreach, or simply showing up to encourage others. When we move from consumers to contributors, our faith deepens, and the church becomes a place of shared purpose.

One church started a "Gift Discovery" workshop, helping members identify their spiritual gifts and find areas to serve. The result was a culture where everyone, from the newest member to the oldest saint, felt valued and equipped to contribute.

Fourth, we can practice radical hospitality. A self-centered church tends to be inward-focused. But when we open our doors, hearts, and tables to others especially those who are different from us we reflect the welcome of Christ. Whether it is greeting newcomers, sharing meals, or creating inclusive spaces, radical hospitality turns a consumer culture into a Christ-centered community.

Fifth, we can challenge the idol of convenience. Faithfulness often requires sacrifice of time, energy, and comfort. Teaching about the cost of discipleship reminds us that following Jesus is not always easy or convenient. Churches can model this by calling members to consistent participation, even when it is inconvenient, and by celebrating stories of sacrificial faith.

I once met a single mother who, despite a long workweek, faithfully volunteered at her church's food pantry every Saturday. When asked why, she simply said, "Because I've been blessed, and I want to give back." Her example challenged others to step beyond convenience into commitment.

Sixth, we can cultivate intergenerational connections. The "Church of Me" often isolates people by age or stage of life. But when generations come together sharing stories, mentoring, worshiping, and serving side by side the focus shifts from self to family. Intergenerational ministries remind us that we belong to something bigger than ourselves.

Seventh, we can embrace spiritual practices that counter consumerism. Regular disciplines like fasting, simplicity, silence, and service help loosen the grip of self-centeredness. Teaching these practices and incorporating them into the life of the church can nurture humility and dependence on God.

Eighth, we must pray for a transformation of hearts. The pull of consumer Christianity is strong, but God's Spirit is stronger. Praying for renewed hearts hearts that look to give rather than receive, to serve rather than be served can unleash a culture shift in the church.

I think of Jesus, who knelt to wash His disciples' feet. In that moment, He embodied the antithesis of the Church of Me. He did not demand to be served; He served. He did not cling to His rights; He laid them down. He did not seek personal comfort; He embraced the cross.

That is the model we are called to follow. When the church embodies that kind of self-giving love, it becomes irresistible not because it caters to our preferences, but because it reflects the heart of God.

The Church of Me may be the dominant culture, but it is not the final word. Together, we can build churches marked by commitment, sacrifice, service, and love a community where Christ is at the center, and every member plays a part.

Chapter Fifteen: The Welcome That Wasn't

It happens quietly, almost imperceptibly. A new family walks into the church on a Sunday morning, a little uncertain, but hopeful. They glance around, wondering where to sit. A greeter hands them a bulletin but does not make eye contact. During the service, they stand for the hymns, sit for the prayers, and try to follow along with unfamiliar customs. At the end, a few polite smiles are offered, but no one stops to introduce themselves or invite them to lunch. They leave feeling invisible.

This is not an isolated story it is one that has repeated itself in churches around the world. The welcome that was not. The church bulletin says, "All are welcome," but the lived experience tells a different story. Visitors feel like outsiders, unsure if they belong, unnoticed by those already settled into familiar circles.

In a culture where loneliness is epidemic and many long for connection, the way a church welcomes or does not welcome visitors can profoundly shape their first impression. A warm greeting can plant the seeds of belonging. An awkward silence or cool reception can drive them away, sometimes for good.

I remember speaking with a couple who had visited five different churches in their search for a new faith community. "At each one," they said, "we felt invisible. People were friendly enough, but no one really engaged with us. We sat alone. We left alone. We finally just gave up."

Why does this happen? How can churches, filled with people of faith and good intentions, fail at one of the most basic expressions of hospitality?

Part of the answer lies in comfort zones. Regular members often gravitate toward friends and familiar faces. They may assume that someone else will greet newcomers or extend an invitation. In larger churches, it is easy to think, "There are so many people here; surely someone else will connect with the visitors." In smaller congregations, members may feel shy or unsure how to approach newcomers.

Another factor is unspoken church culture. While the official message is "All are welcome," the reality may be a tightly knit community where newcomers feel like outsiders peering in. Certain ways of dressing, talking, or taking part may be assumed, leaving visitors feeling out of place.

Then there is the issue of busyness. Sunday mornings can be a whirlwind for church leaders and members alike ushers setting up, musicians rehearsing, children's workers preparing classrooms. Amid the hustle, it is easy to forget that every visitor is someone's opportunity to extend God's love.

But there is a deeper layer still. Sometimes, churches are so focused on keeping their traditions and comfort zones that they unintentionally become insular. They are not hostile they are just inward focused. The idea of welcoming newcomers becomes a slogan rather than a practice.

So, what can we do? How can we ensure that every person who walks through our doors feels seen, valued, and welcomed?

Here are some practical solutions:

First, we must cultivate a culture of hospitality. Hospitality is not just the responsibility of a greeter team it is the calling of every believer. Churches can teach and model hospitality as a spiritual practice, rooted in Scripture. Hebrews 13:2 reminds us, "Do not forget to show hospitality to strangers, for by so doing some people have shown hospitality to angels without knowing it." When hospitality becomes a shared value, it transforms the entire atmosphere.

Second, we can train and empower greeters and ushers. A genuine smile, a warm handshake, and a simple question like, "Is this your first time with us?" can make a world of difference. Training can include how to read body language, how to introduce newcomers to others, and how to follow up with a personal invitation to a future event or small group.

Third, we can intentionally create spaces for connection. Coffee hours, newcomer lunches, and small group gatherings offer low-pressure environments where visitors can meet others and begin to build relationships. These events should be well-publicized and easy to join, with hosts who are trained to be inclusive and attentive.

I recall a church that hosted a monthly "Newcomer's Brunch" where staff and volunteers sat with visitors around tables, shared their own stories of faith, and invited questions. Many first-time guests became regular attendees simply because they felt noticed and valued from the start.

Fourth, we can use simple, intentional language. Instead of saying, "Turn to your neighbor and greet them," leaders can say, "Find someone you don't know yet and introduce yourself." This small shift encourages members to step outside their circles and engage with visitors.

Fifth, we can provide clear signage and instructions. For visitors unfamiliar with the building, obvious signs for parking, restrooms, children's ministries, and worship spaces ease anxiety. A simple announcement explaining the flow of the service can help newcomers feel less disoriented.

Sixth, we can invite visitors into meaningful participation. Instead of relegating them to observer status, invite newcomers to join in whether by standing for a responsive reading, singing with the congregation, or sharing a meal afterward. Participation fosters belonging.

Seventh, we must be patient and persistent. Building a culture of welcome does not happen overnight. It requires ongoing training, reminders, and a willingness to adapt. Leaders should regularly evaluate how welcoming their church truly feels not just to insiders, but to first-time guests.

I think of Jesus' parable of the great banquet in Luke 14. The host sends his servants to invite the poor, the crippled, the blind, and the lame. When there's still room, he sends them out to the roads and country lanes, saying, "Compel them to come in, so that my house will be full." That is the heart of God a radical, inclusive welcome that reaches beyond comfort zones and embraces the stranger.

Eighth, we can foster intergenerational connections. Pairing long-time members with newcomers whether informally or through a "welcome buddy" program can help visitors feel connected and supported. Sharing meals, testimonies, and stories across generations creates a web of belonging.

Ninth, we can pray. Pray for eyes to see the lonely, for hearts to open in compassion, and for God's love to flow through every greeting and conversation. Prayer aligns our hearts with God's and softens the ground for authentic connections.

Finally, we can listen to the stories of those who have felt unwelcome. Their feedback is invaluable. By asking, "What could we have done differently?" we learn and grow. And by responding with humility and grace, we show that we genuinely care.

The welcome that can become the welcome that changes lives. It starts with one handshake, one invitation, one shared story. It grows into a culture where no one feels invisible, where every person who walks through the doors is seen not just as a visitor, but as a beloved child of God.

Chapter Sixteen: The Power of One Invitation

It is easy to think of church growth as a grand strategy marketing campaign, social media promotions, well-produced events but often, the most profound and lasting growth happens one person at a time, through something as simple as a personal invitation.

I remember a young woman named Sarah who told me her story. She was not raised in a church. Her image of Christianity was shaped by media stereotypes and a few distant relatives who occasionally mentioned religion. In college, she met a friend who quietly lived out her faith. One day, the friend simply said, "I am going to Bible study tonight. Want to come with me?"

That small, unassuming question changed Sarah's life. She accepted the invitation, not because she was particularly interested in church, but because she trusted her friend. Over time, the relationships she built in that group, the authenticity she witnessed, and the love she experienced drew her deeper into faith. Today, she is an active leader in her own church community, reaching others with the same kind of invitation.

There is something powerful, almost sacred, about an invitation. It communicates, "I see you. I value you. I want you to be part of something that matters to me." In a world where so many feel unseen and isolated, an invitation offers connection, belonging, and hope.

Yet many of us hesitate. We worry about how the invitation will be received. Will it feel awkward? Will they say no? Will it damage the relationship? These fears often keep us silent, but they should not. Because behind every invitation is the possibility of a life transformed.

I think of the story of Andrew in the Gospel of John. After meeting Jesus, Andrew immediately found his brother Simon Peter and said, "We have found the Messiah!" (John 1:41). He brought Simon to Jesus, and Peter's life and indeed the course of Christian history was forever changed. All because of one invitation.

So, how can we reclaim the power of one invitation in our own lives and churches?

Here are some expanded, practical steps:

First, start with prayer. Ask God to recall specific people in your life neighbors, coworkers, friends, or family members who might be open to an invitation. Pray for their hearts to be softened and for your own courage and sensitivity. Prayer prepares the way for authentic connections

Second, build genuine relationships. Invitations are most effective when they come from a place of relationship. Invest time in getting to know people, listening to their stories, and being present in their lives. When an invitation arises naturally from friendship, it feels less like an agenda and more like an act of love.

I once met a man named Carlos who had attended a church service for the first time in years. When I asked him what brought him, he said, "My neighbor invited me. He has been helping me with yard work, and we talk about life sometimes. One day, he just said, 'Our church is doing a service project this weekend. Want to come?'" That simple, relational invitation made all the difference.

Third, make the invitation clear and simple. Sometimes we overcomplicate it, worrying about how to phrase the question or what to say. But the most effective invitations are straightforward: "Would you like to join me for church on Sunday?" "I am going to Bible study this week. Want to come with me?" "Our church is hosting a community event would you like to check it out?"

It is important to include details—time, location, what to expect so the person feels prepared and comfortable. Offer to meet them outside, sit with them, or introduce them to others to ease any apprehension.

Fourth, do not be discouraged by a "no." Not every invitation will be accepted, and that is okay. The person may not be ready, or there may be other reasons they cannot attend. The important thing is that they know they are valued and welcomed. Sometimes an invitation plants a seed that will bear fruit later.

I think of a woman named Linda who invited her coworker to church multiple times over several years. Each time, her coworker politely declined. Then one day, during a crisis, the coworker reached out, asking, "Is that invitation still open?" It was and it became the beginning of her faith journey.

Fifth, extend invitations to events beyond Sunday services. While worship services are a natural entry point, some people may feel more comfortable attending a special event, service project, or social gathering. Holiday services, concerts, community meals, and family-friendly activities provide opportunities to connect in a less formal setting.

One church I visited hosted an annual "Serve Day," where members volunteered at local schools, food banks, and shelters. Members were encouraged to invite friends, neighbors, and coworkers to join them. Many participants who would not have stepped into a worship service found themselves drawn in by the chance to serve alongside others.

Sixth, train and encourage your congregation. Leaders can model and teach the importance of personal invitations. Sharing testimonies of how simple invitations led to life transformation inspires others to take similar steps. Providing invitation cards, digital resources, or social media templates can equip members to reach out with confidence.

Seventh, create a welcoming culture. An invitation is only the beginning. The experience visitors have when they walk through the doors will determine whether they feel inclined to return. Warm greetings, clear signage, friendly follow-up, and opportunities to connect beyond the first visit create a culture where invitations are not only given but also received with grace.

Eighth, practice patience and persistence. People's openness to spiritual community may change over time. What begins as a "no" today could become a "yes" tomorrow. By continuing to love, serve, and extend invitations, we show the consistent, patient love of Christ.

I think of Jesus' parable in Luke 14, where a host invites guests to a great banquet. When the first guests decline, the host sends servants to invite "the poor, the crippled, the blind, and the lame," and later expands the invitation to "the roads and country lanes." The host's persistence reflects God's heart for inclusion and connection.

Ninth, remember the ripple effect. One invitation can change not just an individual but entire families and communities. When someone accepts an invitation, they may bring their children, spouse, or friends. They may become active participants, volunteers, and leaders, creating ripples of transformation that extend far beyond what we can imagine.

Finally, we must pray for boldness and trust God with the results. Our role is to extend the invitation; the Holy Spirit's role is to work in hearts. When we step out in faith, trusting that God can use our small acts of obedience, we open the door for miracles.

The power of one invitation is not just a strategy it reflects God's heart. He invites us to relationship with Him, and through us, invites others. In a world where many feel unseen and isolated, an invitation says, "You matter. You belong. Come and see."

Chapter Seventeen: The Churches That Are Thriving

In a landscape where many churches struggle with declining attendance and empty pews, there are places sometimes unexpected places where faith communities are flourishing. These churches, large and small, urban, and rural, are not just surviving; they are thriving. Their stories offer hope and practical insights for any congregation seeking renewal.

I think of a vibrant church I visited in a modest neighborhood. The building was simple, the pews well-worn, but the atmosphere was electric. People of all ages filled the sanctuary, their worship heartfelt and their community tightly woven. During the service, several shared testimonies of God's work in their lives. Afterward, the congregation lingered over coffee, sharing stories and laughter. The church was not flashy or wealthy, but it was alive.

So, what makes some churches thrive while others struggle? It is not a matter of luck or perfect leadership. Thriving churches tend to share certain characteristics principles that transcend size, style, and location. Let us explore them, drawing from real-world examples and offering solutions that can inspire any church.

1. Thriving Churches Are Rooted in Prayer

At the heart of every thriving church is a culture of prayer. Prayer is not just a routine it is the fuel for vision, courage, and renewal. Thriving congregations gather for prayer, whether in weekly services, small groups, or special nights of intercession. Leaders model dependence on God, seeking His guidance before launching programs or initiatives.

I visited a church that had a "Prayer Wall" where members posted requests, praises, and answered prayers. This tangible reminder of God's presence kept the congregation connected and expectant. Their Sunday services included extended times of corporate prayer, drawing the congregation together in humility and hope.

Solution: Churches can prioritize prayer by creating dedicated prayer teams, hosting prayer gatherings, and encouraging members to pray regularly for their church, community, and world.

2. Thriving Churches Foster Deep Community

One common thread among thriving churches is an intense sense of belonging. Members know each other, care for one another, and share life's joys and sorrows. This community is often cultivated through small groups, shared meals, service projects, and intergenerational connections.

I recall a church that hosted "Dinner Church" once a month. Tables were set up in the fellowship hall, and members shared a potluck meal, followed by a simple devotional and prayer time. These gatherings broke down barriers and created space for authentic relationships.

Solution: Churches can invest in small groups, mentorship programs, and social gatherings that encourage connection and mutual care.

3. Thriving Churches Have Clear Mission and Vision

A thriving church knows why it exists. Its mission is clear, communicated often, and embraced by the entire congregation. Whether it is making disciples, serving the community, or proclaiming the Gospel, the mission drives decisions, programs, and priorities.

I visited a church whose mission was "Loving God, Loving People, Making a Difference." Every ministry, from children's programs to outreach efforts, aligned with this simple vision. Members were encouraged to find their role in fulfilling the mission, creating a sense of purpose and unity.

Solution: Churches can clarify and communicate their mission, ensuring that every activity aligns with it. Leaders should remind the congregation regularly of the church's purpose and invite them to participate.

4. Thriving Churches Embrace Flexibility and Innovation

Thriving churches are not rigid. They adapt to changing circumstances, experiment with novel approaches, and embrace creativity. Whether it is offering online services, adjusting service times, or reimagining ministry structures, these congregations are willing to change for the sake of the Gospel.

One church in a rural area launched a "Church on the Farm" initiative, holding services outdoors in a barn during the pandemic. The informal setting attracted new families and revitalized the congregation. Another urban church partnered with local businesses to host worship nights in coffee shops and community centers, reaching people who might never set foot in a traditional church.

Solution: Churches can cultivate a culture of flexibility by encouraging innovation, celebrating experimentation, and listening to feedback from the congregation.

5. Thriving Churches Engage the Next Generation

A thriving church invests in its children, youth, and young adults. These congregations provide relevant teaching, mentorship opportunities, and spaces where young people feel seen and valued. They empower young leaders to use their gifts and contribute to the life of the church.

I think of a church that launched a "Youth Apprenticeship" program, pairing teens with mentors in various ministries. From tech teams to hospitality, these young people were trained and given meaningful responsibilities. The result was not only greater engagement from the next generation but also a vibrant sense of ownership and excitement.

Solution: Churches can prioritize youth and children's ministries, create leadership pipelines for young people, and invite them into active participation.

6. Thriving Churches Serve Their Communities

Thriving churches do not exist in isolation they are deeply engaged with their neighborhoods and cities. They host food drives, partner with local schools, provide job training, and offer support to families in need.

This outward focus not only meets practical needs but also builds trust and goodwill.

I visited a church that turned its parking lot into a free farmers' market every Saturday. Volunteers distributed fresh produce, prayed with visitors, and shared information about church services. This simple act of generosity opened doors for ministry and drew people into the congregation.

Solution: Churches can conduct community needs assessments, partner with local organizations, and involve members in service projects that reflect Christ's love.

7. Thriving Churches Are Led with Vision and Humility

Strong, humble leadership is essential for a thriving church. Pastors and ministry leaders who model servant leadership, admit mistakes, and empower others create a culture of trust and collaboration. These leaders seek God's direction and prioritize the spiritual health of their congregations over personal ambition.

I remember a pastor who, during a church meeting, publicly apologized for a decision that had hurt some members. His humility and sincerity defused tension and restored unity. It was a powerful reminder that leadership is about shepherding, not control.

Solution: Churches can invest in leadership development, provide accountability structures, and cultivate a culture of humility and shared responsibility.

8. Thriving Churches Focus on Discipleship

A thriving church does not just attract people it helps them grow. Discipleship is intentional, relational, and integrated into the church's life. Thriving congregations offer classes, mentoring relationships, and spiritual growth opportunities that equip members to live out their faith daily.

One church I visited had a "Discipleship Pathway" with clear steps: starting with exploring faith, then engaging in small groups, serving in ministry, and eventually leading others. This clear, accessible structure gave members a sense of direction and progress in their spiritual journey.

Solution: Churches can develop intentional discipleship plans, offer mentoring opportunities, and provide resources for personal and group growth.

Conclusion: Hope for Every Church

The churches that are thriving are not perfect. They face challenges, conflicts, and setbacks like any congregation. But they share a commitment to prayer, community, mission, innovation, next-generation engagement, community service, humble leadership, and discipleship. These principles are not reserved for large, well-resourced churches they can be embraced by any congregation willing to seek God's vision and step out in faith.

In a world where many churches are struggling, the stories of thriving congregations offer hope. They remind us that God is still at work, that the church is still His instrument of love and transformation, and that renewal is always possible.

Chapter Eighteen: When Faith Feels Fragile

I once sat with a woman who, through tears, confessed, "I am not sure I believe anymore. I still come to church, but it feels like I am just going through the motions." Her words were raw, honest, and echoed the silent struggles of many who fill our pews week after week.

Faith, for many, is not a steady upward climb. It is a journey filled with peaks and valleys, moments of clarity, and seasons of doubt. There are times when God feels close, when Scripture seems alive, when worship stirs the soul. But there are also times sometimes long seasons when faith feels fragile, when prayers feel unanswered, when doubts creep in like shadows.

The pandemic intensified these struggles for many. Isolation, fear, loss, and the disruption of communal worship left countless believers feeling adrift. Some have not returned to church. Others sit quietly, wondering if they belong, feeling ashamed of their questions, or fearing that their doubts make them unworthy.

But here is the truth: fragile faith is still faith. The Bible is filled with stories of people who doubted, wrestled, and questioned. Thomas, often labeled "the doubter," needed to see the wounds before he could believe. Elijah, after his great victory on Mount Carmel, fled in fear and despair, crying out for death. Even Jesus, in Gethsemane, prayed, "Father, if it is possible, let this cup pass from me" (Matthew 26:39).

Doubt and struggle are not signs of failure they are part of the journey. They remind us that faith is not certainty but trust amid uncertainty. They invite us to press deeper, to ask challenging questions, and to seek God's presence even when He feels distant.

So how can the church support those whose faith feels fragile? How can we create communities where questions are welcomed, struggles are shared, and doubts are met with compassion rather than judgment?

Here are some expanded, practical solutions:

1. Create Safe Spaces for Honest Conversations

Many believers feel they must hide their doubts for fear of being judged or seen as "less spiritual." Churches can counter this by creating spaces small groups, discussion forums, or even one-on-one relationships—where honest questions are welcomed. Leaders can model vulnerability by sharing their own struggles, showing that faith is a journey for everyone.

I recall a church that hosted a "Doubt Night," where members gathered to ask problematic questions about faith, Scripture, and life. No answers were off-limits, and the atmosphere was marked by grace and curiosity. Many who attended said it was the first time they felt truly safe to express their doubts.

2. Preach and Teach on Biblical Doubt

The Bible is not a sanitized book of perfect faith it is a collection of stories about real people with real struggles. Preaching and teaching that highlight the doubts and failures of biblical characters can normalize these experiences and offer hope. Sermons on Thomas, Elijah, Job, or the lament psalms remind us that God is not intimidated by our questions.

One pastor I know preached a series titled "When Faith is Hard," exploring themes of doubt, suffering, and silence. The response was overwhelming, as many members felt seen and understood for the first time.

3. Provide Resources for Personal Exploration

Books, podcasts, and study materials on apologetics, spiritual formation, and deconstruction can offer guidance and perspective for those wrestling with their faith. Churches can curate recommended resources and host discussion groups around them, helping members navigate their doubts thoughtfully.

A church I visited started a "Faith in Tension" book club, where members read works by authors who explore faith and doubt. The conversations were deep, honest, and often transformative.

4. Emphasize Community Over Performance

When church feels like a place where everyone must appear "put together," those struggling with doubt feel isolated. Thriving faith communities prioritize relationships over appearances. They create environments where members can say, "I'm not okay," and still be met with love and support.

I think of a small group where a member shared that they were considering leaving the faith altogether. Instead of arguing or shaming, the group listened, prayed, and continued to invite the person into community. Over time, the connection and acceptance rekindled a spark of faith.

5. Offer Pastoral Care and Counseling

Professional counseling or spiritual direction can be invaluable for those navigating deep doubts or spiritual crises. Churches can provide referrals to trusted counselors, offer pastoral care, and ensure that no one walks through their struggle alone.

One church partnered with local Christian counselors to offer free or reduced-cost sessions for members. This practical support acknowledged the emotional and spiritual dimensions of doubt and provided tangible help.

6. Celebrate Small Steps of Faith

For those in a fragile place, attending a service, praying a simple prayer, or opening a Bible can feel like monumental acts of courage. Churches can celebrate these small steps, reminding members that God honors even the tiniest seeds of faith.

One church I know started a practice of "Faith Stories" during services, where members shared brief testimonies of moments when God met them in their doubt. These stories encouraged others and created a culture where imperfect faith was valued.

7. Pray for Strength and Renewal

Prayer is not a last resort it is the foundation of hope. Churches can pray corporately and individually for those struggling with fragile faith.

Prayers for renewal, strength, and encounter with God's love can create an atmosphere where the Spirit moves and restores.

I recall a prayer meeting where members wrote names of friends and family members wrestling with doubt on slips of paper. As they prayed over each name, a deep sense of God's presence and compassion filled the room.

8. Trust the Process of Grace

Finally, we must remember that faith is a work of grace. It is not about perfect understanding or flawless belief it is about responding to God's invitation, even when it feels hard. The church's role is not to "fix" doubters but to walk alongside them, offering love, presence, and hope.

I think of the words of Jude 1:22: "Be merciful to those who doubt." This mercy does not mean offering quick fixes or easy answers. It means holding space for the mystery of faith, trusting that God is at work in ways we may not see.

Conclusion: Fragile but Faithful

When faith feels fragile, it can be tempting to withdraw to stop attending church, to stop praying, to silence the questions. But in those moments, the church's response can make all the difference. By creating spaces of honesty, offering practical support, and extending unwavering love, we can become the hands and feet of Christ to those struggling.

Because in the end, faith is not about how strong we feel it is about holding on, even when we feel weak. And in those moments of fragile faith, we discover the strength of God's grace, which holds us, sustains us, and leads us home.

Chapter Nineteen: When the Pews Fill Again

It was a sight I had not seen in years. The sanctuary was filled not just with a few scattered souls, but with families, couples, teens, and elders all gathered. The murmur of conversations, the laughter of children, the choir practicing in the background it all created a hum of life, of connection. After so many Sundays where empty pews and silence had been the norm, this morning felt like a glimpse of something holy.

But as I stood at the back, watching people stream in, I felt a mixture of emotions. Joy at seeing the community returning. Relief that the long, lonely season of decline was ending. But also caution because I knew that filling the pews was just the beginning. The real work lay ahead.

Too often, churches that experience a sudden increase in attendance whether due to a new pastor, a revival event, a shift in demographics, or simply a cultural moment mistake the surge for long-term renewal. The pews may fill again, but unless the church is prepared to nurture and disciple those who come, the growth can be as fleeting as it is exciting.

I remember a church that, after years of slow decline, saw a sudden influx of young families. The children's ministry tripled overnight. The sanctuary buzzed with energy. But within a year, many of those unfamiliar faces had drifted away. The church had been unprepared to welcome, engage, and disciple them. Programs were stretched thin. Volunteers burned out. Relationships remained surface-level.

The first joy gave way to disappointment and confusion. What had gone wrong?

The truth is that filling pews is not the goal of the church it is a beginning. The real measure of health is not how many seats are occupied, but how many lives are being transformed, how many disciples are being made, how deeply relationships are forming, and how faithfully the church is serving its community.

WHEN THE PEWS GROW EMPTY

So how do we respond when the pews fill again? How do we move from numbers to nourishment, from attendance to authentic engagement?

Reflections

First, we need to recognize that every person who walks through the doors whether for the first time or the hundredth carries a story. Some are seekers, curious but cautious. Others are long-time believers returning after a season of drift. Some are wounded by past church experiences and are testing the waters again. Others are looking for community, meaning, or simply a place to belong.

I spoke with a young couple who had returned to church after a decade away. "We're here because we need something solid," they said. "But we are not sure we will stay. We want to know if this is real if it is more than just a show." Their words reminded me that filling pews is not about entertainment or numbers it is about creating space where people can encounter the living God and be embraced by a genuine community.

Another man I met had joined a church during a revival event. "It was exciting at first," he shared, "but after a few weeks, no one followed up. I felt like I was just another face in the crowd. Eventually, I stopped coming." His story echoes a truth many churches must face connection does not happen by accident. It requires intentionality, follow-up, and a culture of care.

The Opportunity

When the pews fill again, it is a moment of opportunity. It is a chance to reevaluate systems, invest in relationships, and refocus on the church's mission. It is a time to ask:

- Are we prepared to disciple new believers?
- Do we have systems in place to connect visitors to small groups and service opportunities?
- Are we equipping leaders to care for a growing congregation?
- Are we cultivating a culture where people are known, valued,

and encouraged to grow?

The answer to these questions decides whether the resurgence leads to long-term health or a temporary spike.

I think of the parable of the sower in Matthew 13. Seeds scattered on rocky soil sprang up quickly but withered because they had no root. In contrast, seeds on good soil grew deep roots and produced lasting fruit. The task of the church is not just to scatter invitations but to cultivate the soil, to nurture growth, and to walk alongside people as they deepen their roots of faith.

Solutions

Here are practical solutions for when the pews fill again:

- Develop a follow-up system. Ensure that visitors and new attendees are welcomed personally, followed up with during the week, and invited into smaller gatherings where relationships can form. Assign teams or individuals to connect with newcomers, answer questions, and offer guidance.
- Expand small groups. Create or strengthen small group ministries that provide space for deeper connection and spiritual growth. Equip and train small group leaders to shepherd these groups well.
- Invest in discipleship pathways. Offer clear steps for people to move from attending to belonging and from exploring faith to serving and leading. This might include classes, mentoring relationships, or ministry opportunities that align with the church's mission.
- Equip volunteers and leaders. A growing congregation needs a growing team of leaders and volunteers. Provide training, resources, and support to prevent burnout and ensure that ministries can scale effectively.
- Strengthen communication. Clearly communicate

opportunities for connection, service, and growth through bulletins, announcements, social media, and personal invitations. Make sure people know how to take the next step.
- Prioritize personal relationships. Beyond programs and events, encourage members to reach out to newcomers—inviting them to lunch, sharing stories, and offering a listening ear. Relationships are the heart of a thriving church.
- Stay rooted in prayer and Scripture. As attendance grows, guard against the temptation to focus on numbers alone. Keep the church centered on Christ through corporate prayer, faithful preaching, and a commitment to biblical discipleship.
- Anticipate growing pains. Recognize that growth brings challenges—logistical, relational, and spiritual. Approach these challenges with flexibility, grace, and a focus on long-term health rather than short-term success.
- Celebrate milestones. Mark moments of growth and transformation with celebrations—baptisms, testimonies, volunteer appreciation, and community gatherings. Celebrate not just the numbers, but the stories of lives changed by God's grace.

When the pews fill again, it is a reminder that God is still at work, drawing people into His family. But it is also a call to action a call to move beyond surface-level engagement into the deeper waters of authentic community, discipleship, and mission.

Chapter Twenty: A New Beginning

It was early one Sunday morning when I arrived at the church a place that had seen both fullness and emptiness, hope and discouragement. The sanctuary lights were just coming on, the air still carrying the faint scent of last week's flowers. As I sat quietly in a pew, I thought about the journey this congregation and many others like it had traveled. Years of growth and decline. Moments of division and unity. Seasons of thriving and struggling. But here, in the stillness, was a new sense of anticipation.

This was more than just another Sunday. It was a new beginning.

For many churches, the story does not end when attendance drops or when conflict seems insurmountable. It does not end when the pews empty or when budgets tighten. Instead, those moments become thresholds opportunities to rediscover what it means to be the church, to lean into God's faithfulness, and to begin anew.

I have seen this renewal firsthand. I have seen congregations that, after years of stagnation, embraced fresh vision and purpose. I have seen churches once divided by worship wars come together in unity and grace. I have seen new believers walk through the doors, drawn not by programs or productions but by the simple, authentic love of a community committed to Christ.

A new beginning is not about flashy marketing or clever strategies. It is about returning to the heart of what makes the church the church: prayer, worship, discipleship, service, and love. It is about remembering that the church exists not for itself, but to be a light in the world, a reflection of God's kingdom on earth.

A Shift in Mindset

For many congregations, embracing a new beginning requires a shift in mindset. It means moving from scarcity thinking focusing on what we lack to abundance thinking, recognizing the resources God has already provided. It means shifting from inward focus protecting our comfort and preferences to outward focus, serving the needs of the community.

I remember a pastor who, after years of decline in his church, gathered his leadership team and posed a question: "If our church closed its doors tomorrow, would our community notice?" The question led to a season of prayer, reflection, and eventually, action. The church launched a food pantry, partnered with local schools, and opened its building for community events. Slowly, the congregation grew not just in numbers, but in purpose.

A new beginning often starts with a simple but profound decision: to trust God for the future.

Embracing Change with Courage

Change is never easy. It challenges our routines, our assumptions, and sometimes, our very identity. But when approached with courage and prayerful discernment, change can be a catalyst for renewal.

I recall a congregation that faced the difficult decision to sell their aging building and move into a shared community space. At first, there was resistance. The building had been their spiritual home for generations. But as they embraced the change, they discovered new opportunities for outreach, deeper relationships, and a renewed sense of mission. They realized that the church is not a building it is the people.

For some churches, change might mean rethinking worship styles, reevaluating ministries, or embracing new leadership. For others, it might mean letting go of outdated programs to focus on what truly matters: making disciples, serving neighbors, and loving God wholeheartedly.

Anchoring in Scripture and Prayer

A true new beginning is not driven by human ambition, but by God's Word and Spirit. Thriving churches ground themselves in Scripture, seeking wisdom, guidance, and encouragement. They prioritize prayer not as an afterthought, but as the foundation of everything they do.

One church I visited began each new initiative with a 40-day season of prayer and fasting. Members gathered in homes and in the sanctuary to seek God's direction. Leaders listened for the Spirit's prompting. As a result, decisions were made not out of anxiety or pressure, but from a place of peace and clarity.

Prayer aligns hearts with God's purposes. It softens resistance, kindles vision, and empowers action. Scripture provides the blueprint for a church that reflects Christ's love and mission.

Celebrating Small Steps

A new beginning is not always marked by dramatic change or immediate growth. Often, it is found in small, faithful steps a family returning after years away, a new believer being baptized, a hesitant volunteer stepping forward to serve. Each of these moments is a testimony to God's ongoing work.

I think of a church that celebrated its first baby dedication in years. The entire congregation gathered around the young family, praying over them and pledging support. It was not just a milestone for the family it was a sign of hope for the church's future.

Celebrating these moments reinforces a culture of gratitude and attentiveness to God's faithfulness. It reminds the congregation that renewal is not just about numbers, but about lives transformed by grace.

Building for the Future

A new beginning also involves intentional planning for the future. Thriving churches develop leadership pipelines, mentor emerging leaders, and invest in ministries that will outlast current trends. They ask awkward questions:

- How are we preparing the next generation?
- How are we equipping members to live out their faith daily?
- How are we serving not just our congregation, but our community and beyond?

One church started a leadership development program that paired younger members with seasoned mentors. Together, they studied Scripture, prayed, and served in various ministries. Over time, these emerging leaders brought fresh energy and ideas to the congregation, ensuring continuity and vitality.

Staying Rooted in Love

At the heart of any new beginning is love. Love for God, love for one another, love for neighbor. Without love, even the most innovative strategies or dynamic programs will fall flat.

I am reminded of Paul's words in 1 Corinthians 13: "If I speak in the tongues of men or of angels, but do not have love, I am only a resounding gong or a clanging cymbal." Love is what gives the church its true identity and witness.

When a congregation loves well—welcoming the stranger, serving the hurting, forgiving the offender—it becomes a beacon of hope in a broken world. It becomes a place where people meet not just a religious service, but the living Christ.

Solutions for a New Beginning

Here are practical solutions to embrace a new beginning:

- Pray intentionally. Begin with a season of prayer, inviting the entire congregation to seek God's guidance and renewal.
- Clarify mission and vision. Rearticulate the church's purpose, focusing on biblical principles and the unique calling of the congregation.
- Engage the community. Develop partnerships with local organizations, host events, and meet practical needs to build trust and relevance.
- Invest in leadership development. Mentor emerging leaders, provide training, and encourage shared leadership models.
- Foster authentic relationships. Create small groups, mentoring programs, and service teams where people can connect deeply and grow together.
- Celebrate milestones. Acknowledge and honor moments of growth, commitment, and transformation to encourage the

congregation.
- Stay adaptable. Remain open to change, willing to adjust methods and structures to serve the mission effectively.
- Keep love at the center. Let every decision, program, and interaction be guided by a heart of love for God and neighbor.

Conclusion: Hope for Tomorrow

A new beginning does not erase the past. It honors the journey, learns from missteps, and embraces the present with hope. It is a testament to God's faithfulness, a commitment to growth, and an invitation to step into His unfolding story.

As I left that sanctuary that morning, watching the sunlight pour through the stained glass, I was reminded that the church is not a building or a program. It is a living body, made up of imperfect people drawn together by the love of Christ. No matter how empty the pews have been, no matter how broken the past, there is always room for a new beginning.

Because God is not done with His church.

Final Chapter: Bringing It All Together Insights and Solutions

As we come to the close of this journey through the challenges and possibilities facing today's churches, we pause to reflect on what we have uncovered. From empty pews to doctrinal disputes, from digital dilemmas to fragile faith, the story has been one of both struggle and hope. This book has not shied away from the hard truths, but it has also illuminated pathways toward renewal, rooted in prayer, love, and God's enduring faithfulness.

What follows is a comprehensive summary of each chapter, highlighting its core message and offering practical solutions for churches and believers longing for a new beginning.

Chapter One: The Echo of Silence

We began in an empty sanctuary, reflecting on the silence left by declining attendance. The question arose: Could these pews be filled again? The silence was not the end it was an invitation to listen to the Spirit, to face hard truths, and to begin anew.

Solutions:

- Acknowledge the reality of decline with honesty and compassion.
- Listen deeply to the reasons people leave whether hurt, busyness, or spiritual disconnection.
- Begin with prayer, inviting God to guide the church's renewal.

Chapter Two: Remembering the Why

Churches often lose sight of their mission in the busyness of programs and traditions. This chapter called us to return to the core purpose: to glorify God, make disciples, and serve the world in love.

Solutions:

- Rearticulate the church's mission and values, ensuring they align with Scripture.
- Share stories of lives changed by faith to inspire and reorient the congregation.
- Evaluate programs and practices considering the church's core mission.

Chapter Three: The Lost Generations

Younger generations are increasingly absent from church life. Their departure is often tied to perceived irrelevance, hypocrisy, and a lack of authentic relationships. But the door is not closed churches can reengage them through intentional, relational ministry.

Solutions:

- Create spaces for honest questions and conversations about faith.
- Empower young people to lead and contribute, valuing their gifts and perspectives.
- Foster mentoring relationships that connect generations.

Chapter Four: Digital Dilemma

Technology, especially after the pandemic, has become both a blessing and a challenge. Digital ministry can reach beyond walls, but it cannot replace embodied community.

Solutions:

- Use digital tools to complement, not replace, in-person worship.
- Engage online participants with interactive opportunities.
- Encourage hybrid models that include and value both in-person and digital participants.

Chapter Five: Pastor Burnout and Pulpit Fatigue

Pastors and leaders are often overwhelmed by unrealistic expectations and isolation. Burnout erodes the health of both the leader and the church.
Solutions:

- Encourage pastors to take regular sabbath and sabbaticals.
- Develop lay leadership to share the load.
- Create safe spaces for pastors to be vulnerable and receive support.

Chapter Six: Community Without a Sanctuary
Some churches have lost their buildings or chosen to leave them. But the church is not a structure; it is the people of God.
Solutions:

- Reimagine church in homes, parks, or community spaces.
- Prioritize relationships and shared mission over physical spaces.
- Embrace flexibility and creativity in gathering.

Chapter Seven: The Missing Men
Men's absence from church life is both visible and concerning. Yet men, too, are seeking purpose, connection, and challenge.
Solutions:

- Offer ministry opportunities that engage men's interests and strengths.
- Develop mentorship programs where older men invest in younger ones.
- Foster a culture of authenticity where men can be vulnerable and grow.

Chapter Eight: Worship Wars

Conflicts over worship style can fracture churches. The focus must shift from preference to purpose worship that glorifies God and draws people into His presence.

Solutions:

- Embrace blended worship styles that honor tradition and innovation.
- Focus on the theological depth of songs rather than their style.
- Create opportunities for congregational input and understanding.

Chapter Nine: Faith in a Post-Pandemic World

The pandemic left many spiritually disconnected and uncertain. Yet it also opened doors for creativity, resilience, and new ways of being church.

Solutions:

- Acknowledge collective grief and offer spaces for lament and healing.
- Embrace hybrid church models and flexible gathering options.
- Simplify church life to focus on relationships and discipleship.

Chapter Ten: Doctrine Wars and Denominational Division

Theological disagreements have divided many churches. Yet unity does not require uniformity; it requires humility, love, and a shared commitment to the Gospel.

Solutions:

- Prioritize core doctrines over secondary issues.
- Create forums for respectful dialogue.
- Foster relationships across denominational lines.

Chapter Eleven: The Welcome That Was not

Many visitors leave churches feeling invisible or unwelcome. Hospitality must move from theory to practice.
Solutions:

- Train greeters and members to engage warmly with visitors.
- Create intentional spaces for connection, such as newcomer lunches or coffee hours.
- Follow up personally with guests to invite them into community.

Chapter Twelve: The Power of One Invitation
Church growth often starts with one invitation. Personal connections open doors to faith.
Solutions:

- Encourage members to pray for and invite friends and neighbors.
- Provide clear, simple invitation tools and resources.
- Celebrate stories of transformation sparked by invitations.

Chapter Thirteen: The Churches That Are Thriving
Thriving churches share common traits: prayer, community, mission, flexibility, intergenerational engagement, service, humble leadership, and discipleship.
Solutions:

- Cultivate a culture of prayer.
- Foster deep, authentic community.
- Equip leaders and prioritize outreach and service.

Chapter Fourteen: The Church of Me
Consumerism has shaped many churches, turning faith into a transaction. The antidote is a return to commitment, service, and love.

Solutions:

- Teach the value of commitment and perseverance.
- Encourage members to shift from consumers to contributors.
- Foster intergenerational connections and shared service.

Chapter Fifteen: When Faith Feels Fragile
Doubt and struggle are part of the journey. The church must become a place where questions are welcomed, and support is offered.

Solutions:

- Create safe spaces for honest conversations.
- Teach and preach on biblical examples of doubt.
- Provide pastoral care, resources, and prayer for those struggling.

Chapter Sixteen: When the Pews Fill Again
When attendance rises, the real work begins nurturing, connecting, and discipling those who come.
Solutions:

- Develop follow-up systems and small groups.
- Invest in discipleship pathways and leadership development.
- Celebrate growth and focus on long-term health over numbers.

Chapter Seventeen: A New Beginning
The journey concludes with hope. The church's future is not figured out by its past but by its willingness to embrace God's calling with courage and love.
Solutions:

- Pray intentionally for vision and renewal.
- Clarify mission and vision.
- Invest in community engagement, leadership, and relationships.
- Keep Christ's love at the center of everything.

Conclusion:
This book has traced a journey from silence to hope, from struggle to renewal. The solutions offered are not quick fixes but pathways that require prayer, humility, perseverance, and love. Every church no matter its size, location, or history can begin anew.

The question is not if God will work through His people, but when and how we will respond to His call. Will we listen to the echoes of silence and respond with faith? Will we welcome the missing, embrace change, foster community, and love deeply?

This is the invitation. This is the challenge. This is the opportunity for every church—to become a beacon of hope, a refuge of grace, and a living testimony to the enduring love of Christ.

Chapter 18: When Faith Feels Fragile

This chapter acknowledged the struggles many believers face during seasons of doubt, uncertainty, and silence. Faith is not a steady climb it involves valleys of questions and moments of spiritual dryness. The church's role is to support, not shame, those whose faith feels fragile.

Solutions:

- Create safe spaces for honest conversations about doubt and struggle.
- Preach and teach on biblical examples of doubt to normalize the experience.
- Provide pastoral care, counseling, and spiritual direction.
- Offer resources and small groups focused on navigating doubt.
- Celebrate small steps of faith and pray intentionally for those in fragile places.

Chapter 19: When the Pews Fill Again

This chapter reflected on what happens when attendance surges whether through revival, cultural shifts, or renewed interest. It emphasized that filling pews is just the beginning; nurturing faith, discipleship, and connection must follow.

Solutions:

- Develop a strong follow-up system for visitors and new attendees.
- Expand small groups and mentorship opportunities.
- Provide clear discipleship pathways and ministry opportunities.
- Train and support volunteers and leaders to handle growth.
- Maintain a focus on relationships and prayerful dependence on God.
- Celebrate milestones while planning for sustainable, long-term health.

Chapter 20: A New Beginning

The journey concluded with a message of hope and renewal. The church's future is not figured out by past failures but by its willingness to embrace God's calling with courage, love, and faith. A new beginning is possible when churches return to core practices: prayer, worship, community, service, and love.

Solutions:

- Begin with a season of prayer, seeking God's vision and direction.
- Rearticulate the church's mission and vision, focusing on biblical values.
- Engage the surrounding community through service and outreach.
- Invest in leadership development and mentoring.
- Cultivate authentic relationships and small groups for deeper connection.
- Celebrate every step of renewal and transformation, no matter how small.
- Keep love at the center of every decision, plan, and interaction.

About the Author

Edward Fair's life is a profound testament to the power of resilience, faith, and the transformative work of the Holy Spirit. Born in Ohio 66 years ago with blindness in his right eye due to an underdeveloped optic nerve, Edward's journey has been marked by overcoming obstacles that might have discouraged many. Yet through God's grace, he embraced a calling to serve others a calling that has led him to touch countless lives as a paramedic, firefighter, educator, Certified Lay Minister, and a servant of Christ.

His ministry began in earnest during his youth when he immersed himself in church life. As a youth director, Edward led young hearts toward Christ, creating a nurturing environment where the Holy Spirit's presence could be felt. His work did not stop there he served faithfully on the church council and in various ministry committees, lending his voice to decisions that shaped the church's direction and outreach. These experiences deepened his understanding of the challenges facing modern churches and the desperate need for Spirit-led renewal.

Throughout his ministry, Edward has preached on faith, drawing from firsthand experiences and Scripture to encourage congregations to trust in God's power. His sermons often include stories that, while they may sound impossible to human ears, are undeniable testaments to the truth that "nothing is impossible with God" (Luke 1:37).

Edward recalls preaching about moments when desperate prayers were answered in ways that defied logic. He shared stories of miraculous healings, moments when God's provision arrived just in time, and instances when the Holy Spirit moved through worship so powerfully that lives were forever changed. These stories were not told to entertain but to awaken faith to remind listeners that God is not confined by our human understanding or limitations.

One of Edward's most memorable sermon themes focused on the truth Jesus shared with his disciples in John's Gospel:

> "Jesus looked at them and said, 'With man this is impossible, but with God all things are possible.'" (Matthew 19:26, echoed in John 14:12-14)

In these messages, Edward emphasized that the impossible becomes possible not through human effort but by the Spirit's power. He often concluded such sermons with a challenge: What impossible thing is God calling you to believe for today?

These experiences shaped Edward's vision for the church. He witnessed congregations busy with programs and attendance goals but lacking the transforming presence of the Holy Spirit. It was this burden that inspired When the Pews Grow Empty. In it, Edward calls on readers, church leaders, and communities to reawaken their dependence on the Spirit to move beyond empty rituals and embrace a living, dynamic faith.

As Jesus promised:

> "But you will receive power when the Holy Spirit comes on you; and you will be my witnesses in Jerusalem, and in all Judea and Samaria, and to the ends of the earth." (Acts 1:8)

Edward's life reflects this promise. His service as a paramedic and firefighter prepared him for ministry in unexpected ways. The urgency of emergency response taught him the value of decisive faith, the need to rely on more than just human strength. It was often in those crisis moments that he learned to trust the leading of the Spirit, to pray for wisdom beyond his understanding, and to bear witness to the miracles God can perform.

Now, at age 66, Edward continues to live out his calling as a Certified Lay Minister in the United Methodist Church. His teaching and preaching have touched many, whether through local church services, special events, or his books, including Through the Flames, The

Christmas Bell Ringer, and One Good Eye, One Blind. Each work carries the theme of hope, resilience, and the transformative power of God's love.

In When the Pews Grow Empty, Edward invites readers to pause and reflect on the true state of their churches and their own hearts. He does not shy away from the challenging questions: Where is the Spirit moving? Are we relying on our own strength or surrendering to God's power? He reminds us that the early church thrived not because of perfect programs but because the Spirit was alive and active among them.

"The wind blows wherever it pleases. You hear its sound, but you cannot tell where it comes from or where it is going. So, it is with everyone born of the Spirit." (John 3:8)

Edward longs to see the modern church reclaim that same vitality. He envisions communities where worship is not a routine but a radical encounter with God; where prayer is fervent, bold, and expectant; where believers are empowered to step out in faith, knowing the Spirit will guide and provide. His life and ministry echo Jesus' words:

"Very truly I tell you, whoever believes in me will do the works I have been doing, and they will do even greater things than these, because I am going to the Father. And I will do whatever you ask in my name, so that the Father may be glorified in the Son." (John 14:12-13)

Edward continues to live in Hermitage, Pennsylvania, where he stays an active participant in his church community. Whether leading worship, teaching classes, or encouraging fellow believers, he brings a message of hope and a deep conviction that God is not done with His church.

He often reflects on the powerful truth that God's Spirit can work through anyone a truth he embodies in his own journey from a young boy navigating monocular vision to a minister of the Gospel. His ministry is a living witness that the impossible becomes possible when we yield to the Holy Spirit's leading.

Edward's life story and preaching invite readers to believe again to expect miracles, to pray bold prayers, and to step into the impossible with confidence. As he often tells his congregations: It may sound impossible, but with Jesus and the Holy Spirit, nothing is beyond reach.

"But the Advocate, the Holy Spirit, whom the Father will send in my name, will teach you all things and will remind you of everything I have said to you." (John 14:26)

"Peace, I leave with you; my peace I give you. I do not give to you as the world gives. Do not let your hearts be troubled and do not be afraid." (John 14:27)

In When the Pews Grow Empty, Edward's challenge is clear: let us not settle for empty pews and lifeless worship. Let us embrace the power of the Spirit, trusting that what seems impossible to man is more than possible with God.

www.ingramcontent.com/pod-product-compliance
Lightning Source LLC
Chambersburg PA
CBHW032149040426
42449CB00005B/457